Blazor Quick Start Guide

Build web applications using Blazor, EF Core, and SQL Server

Ankit Sharma

BIRMINGHAM - MUMBAI

Blazor Quick Start Guide

Copyright © 2018 Packt Publishing

Commissioning Editor: Kunal Chaudhari
Acquisition Editor: Reshma Raman
Content Development Editor: Mohammed Yusuf Imaratwale
Technical Editor: Jinesh Topiwala
Copy Editor: Safis Editing
Project Coordinator: Hardik Bhinde
Proofreader: Safis Editing
Indexer: Priyanka Dhadke
Graphics: Alishon Mendonsa
Production Coordinator: Shraddha Falebhai

First published: October 2018

Production reference: 211118

Published by Packt Publishing Ltd.
Livery Place
35 Livery Street
Birmingham
B3 2PB, UK.

ISBN 978-1-78934-414-1

www.packtpub.com

To my mother, Vibha Sharma, for everything she did for me.

– Ankit Sharma

`mapt.io`

Mapt is an online digital library that gives you full access to over 5,000 books and videos, as well as industry leading tools to help you plan your personal development and advance your career. For more information, please visit our website.

Why subscribe?

- Spend less time learning and more time coding with practical eBooks and Videos from over 4,000 industry professionals

- Improve your learning with Skill Plans built especially for you

- Get a free eBook or video every month

- Mapt is fully searchable

- Copy and paste, print, and bookmark content

Packt.com

Did you know that Packt offers eBook versions of every book published, with PDF and ePub files available? You can upgrade to the eBook version at `www.packt.com` and as a print book customer, you are entitled to a discount on the eBook copy. Get in touch with us at `customercare@packtpub.com` for more details.

At `www.packt.com`, you can also read a collection of free technical articles, sign up for a range of free newsletters, and receive exclusive discounts and offers on Packt books and eBooks.

Foreword

.NET has been around for a decade now, and Blazor uses all goodness of .NET to create a Single Page web application. It is a single-page web app framework built on .NET that runs on the browser with WebAssembly. If you are wondering how .NET can run browsers; well, that is possible through this new technology called WebAssesmbly. Code compiled with WebAssembly can run on any browser with a native speed.

In my opinion, every web developer should learn Blazor, and Ankit has done good justice to the subject for beginners. There are seven chapters in this book, which cover everything you need to know, right from the basics to the deployment of Single Page Application created in Blazor.

Lastly, I congratulate Ankit for writing such a detailed book on such a new technology Blazor.

– Dhananjay Kumar

9 times Microsoft MVP, Developer Evangelist for Infragistics and founder of geek97. He organizes India's Angular Conference ng-India. Tweet him @debug_mode

Contributors

About the author

Ankit Sharma is a software engineer currently working with IVY Comptech in Hyderabad, India. He acquired a bachelor's degree in computer science from Siddaganga Institute of Technology, Karnataka, in 2014. He has over four years of extensive experience in Microsoft technologies, including C#, ASP.NET, and SQL Server, as well as in UI technologies, such as jQuery and Angular.

Ankit is a technical author and speaker who loves to contribute to the technical community. He writes articles for multiple platforms, including C# Corner, DZone, Medium, and TechNet Wiki. For his dedicated contribution to the developer community, he has been recognized as a C# Corner MVP, a DZone MVB, and a Top Contributor in Technology at Medium. You can tweet him @ankitsharma_007.

I would like to thank my mother for her continuous support throughout the proces of writing this book.
I would also like to thank my friends, Dhiraj and Rahul, for their ideas and feedback on the technical aspects of this book.

About the reviewer

Sarath Lal is a passionate software developer who has more than 10 years' experience in the software industry. He possess strong experience in web and Windows development using .Net technologies such as ASP.Net Web forms, MVC, and Web API. He is well versed with C, HTML, C #, .Net, CSS, JavaScript, jQuery, AngularJS, Angular 6, Python, and Cosmos DB.

He is an excellent communicator, articulate, combined with strong business acumen and logical approach, an ability to handle multiple functions and activities in high pressure environments with tight deadlines.

He is always enthusiastic in learning new things along with sharing his knowledge through various communities like C# Corner and Codeproject.

Syed Shanu is a three-time Microsoft MVP, a four-time C# Corner MVP, and four-time Code project MVP. Shanu is also an author, blogger, and speaker. He's from Madurai, Tamil Nadu, India, and works as technical lead in South Korea. With more than 11 years of experience with Microsoft technologies, Shanu is an active person in the community and always happy to share his knowledge on topics related to ASP.NET (http://asp.net/), MVC, ASP.NET Core , Web API, SQL Server, Angular, ASP.NET Core Blazor, among others. He has written more than 100 articles on various technologies. He's also a several-time TechNet Guru Gold Winner. Follow him on Twitter @syedshanu3.

Packt is searching for authors like you

If you're interested in becoming an author for Packt, please visit authors.packtpub.com and apply today. We have worked with thousands of developers and tech professionals, just like you, to help them share their insight with the global tech community. You can make a general application, apply for a specific hot topic that we are recruiting an author for, or submit your own idea.

Table of Contents

Preface

Modern web applications are more inclined toward using a client-side framework than a server-side one. Some of the popular options available to us include Angular, React.js, and Vue.js. All of these use JavaScript or TypeScript (a superset of JavaScript) as their scripting language. However, moving to a client-side framework from a server-side technology, such as C#, requires learning a new JavaScript framework. This demands a substantial amount of time and training resources.

Blazor is an open source .NET web framework based on C#/Razor and HTML that runs in the browser with WebAssembly. It simplifies web development by allowing us to write .NET-based web apps that run client-side in web browsers. This alleviates the problem of moving to a new JavaScript framework. We can take advantage of the existing knowledge of C# to write both client-side and server-side applications and have a full-stack .NET development experience.

In this book, we will explore the Blazor framework. We will touch upon the following points:

- What Blazor is and how it works
- The advantages of the Blazor framework
- The core concepts of Blazor, such as Blazor components, data binding, dependency injection, routing, and JavaScript interop
- How to create a **Single Page Application (SPA)** using Blazor
- How to use Entity Framework Core and ADO.NET with Blazor
- Deploying a Blazor application on IIS and Azure

By the end of this book, you will have mastered the Blazor framework and will be able to create rich and interactive web applications using Blazor as a frontend and SQL Server as the database provider.

Who this book is for

If you are working in a .NET environment, then ask yourself these questions:

- Do you want to use a client-side framework in your web application?
- Are you comfortable with C# and struggling to migrate to JavaScript-based frameworks?
- Do you want to have a full-stack .NET experience in your application?

 If the answer to these questions is **yes**, then this book is for you.

What this book covers

Chapter 1, *An Introduction to Blazor*, looks at what Blazor is and how it works. We will create our first Blazor application using Visual Studio Code and the **Command-Line Interface (CLI)**.

Chapter 2, *Exploring Blazor Concepts*, explores the building blocks of the Blazor framework, including Blazor components, data binding, layouts, event handling, dependency injection, Blazor routing, and the life cycle methods of Blazor.

Chapter 3, *A Deep-Diving into JavaScript Interop*, covers JavaScript interop, one of the important features of Blazor. We will examine JavaScript interop and how to call a JavaScript function from C# and vice versa.

Chapter 4, *Getting Started with Blazor Using Visual Studio 2017*, has you set up the Blazor development environment using Visual Studio 2017. We will also create two client-side applications using Blazor: a Tic-Tac-Toe game and a basic calculator.

Chapter 5, *Creating a Single Page Application Using Blazor*, is where we will start creating an ASP.NET Core-hosted Blazor application. In this chapter, we will create the server part of the application. We will explore two different methods for handling database interaction in a Blazor application: one using Entity Framework Core and another using ADO.NET.

Chapter 6, *Extending Your Application*, continues with the application started in the previous chapter, looking at finishing the client side of things. We will also see the execution demo of our app.

Chapter 7, *Hosting and Deployment*, teaches you how to deploy a Blazor application on IIS and Azure.

To get the most out of this book

Before starting this book, you must have the following skills:

- A basic understanding of the .NET Core framework in general and ASP.NET Core in particular
- A working knowledge of the web development process
- A good understanding of the C# language
- A basic understanding of Entity Framework Core and ADO.NET concepts

Download the example code files

You can download the example code files for this book from your account at www.packt.com. If you purchased this book elsewhere, you can visit www.packt.com/support and register to have the files emailed directly to you.

You can download the code files by following these steps:

1. Log in or register at www.packt.com.
2. Select the **SUPPORT** tab.
3. Click on **Code Downloads & Errata**.
4. Enter the name of the book in the **Search** box and follow the onscreen instructions.

Once the file is downloaded, please make sure that you unzip or extract the folder using the latest version of:

- WinRAR/7-Zip for Windows
- Zipeg/iZip/UnRarX for Mac
- 7-Zip/PeaZip for Linux

The code bundle for the book is also hosted on GitHub at https://github.com/PacktPublishing/Blazor-Quick-Start-Guide. In case there's an update to the code, it will be updated on the existing GitHub repository.

We also have other code bundles from our rich catalog of books and videos available at https://github.com/PacktPublishing/. Check them out!

Code in action

Visit the following link to check out videos of the code being run:

`http://bit.ly/2RmLhOM`

Conventions used

There are a number of text conventions used throughout this book.

`CodeInText`: Indicates code words in text, database table names, folder names, filenames, file extensions, pathnames, dummy URLs, user input, and Twitter handles. Here is an example: "The `RenderFragment` parameter will be provided between the tags to the child component."

A block of code is set as follows:

```
<li class="nav-item px-3">
<NavLink class="nav-link" href="singlepagecomp">
<span class="oi oi-list-rich" aria-hidden="true"></span> Comp Demo
</NavLink>
</li>
```

Bold: Indicates a new term, an important word, or words that you see onscreen. For example, words in menus or dialog boxes appear in the text like this. Here is an example: "An **Add New Item** dialog box will open, asking you to select the desired item template from the provided list of items."

Warnings or important notes appear like this.

Tips and tricks appear like this.

Get in touch

Feedback from our readers is always welcome.

General feedback: If you have questions about any aspect of this book, mention the book title in the subject of your message and email us at customercare@packtpub.com.

Errata: Although we have taken every care to ensure the accuracy of our content, mistakes do happen. If you have found a mistake in this book, we would be grateful if you would report this to us. Please visit www.packt.com/submit-errata, selecting your book, clicking on the Errata Submission Form link, and entering the details.

Piracy: If you come across any illegal copies of our works in any form on the Internet, we would be grateful if you would provide us with the location address or website name. Please contact us at copyright@packt.com with a link to the material.

If you are interested in becoming an author: If there is a topic that you have expertise in and you are interested in either writing or contributing to a book, please visit authors.packtpub.com.

Reviews

Please leave a review. Once you have read and used this book, why not leave a review on the site that you purchased it from? Potential readers can then see and use your unbiased opinion to make purchase decisions, we at Packt can understand what you think about our products, and our authors can see your feedback on their book. Thank you!

For more information about Packt, please visit packt.com.

An Introduction to Blazor 1

Modern web applications have two parts: client side and server side. The client side of the application is mostly developed using UI frameworks, such as Angular or React, which use JavaScript or Typescript as their preferred language. The server side of the application is created using frameworks such as .NET, using languages such as C#. However, switching between two different frameworks and languages is sometimes cumbersome. Also, moving from C# to JavaScript is a bit time-consuming, given the fact that mastering JavaScript involves a steep learning curve.

Blazor provides us with the facility to write both the client side and server side of the application using C#. We can create a rich and modern **Single Page Application (SPA)** with the Blazor framework, using only the C# language, and run it on the browser of our choice.

In this chapter, we will explore the following points:

- What is Blazor?
- How does Blazor work?
- Why should we use Blazor?

We will also create our first Blazor application using Visual Studio Code and the **Command-Line Interface (CLI)**.

Technical requirements

You need to have knowledge on following concepts:

- C#
- ASP.NET Core
- Entity Framework Core
- Ado.NET

You should also install following software to start Blazor development.

- .NET Core 2.1 or above SDK.
- Visual Studio Code
- Visual Studio 2017 v15.7 or above
- ASP.NET Core Blazor Language Services extension

The code files of this chapter can be found on GitHub:
`https://github.com/PacktPublishing/Blazor-Quick-Start-Guide/tree/master/`
`Chapter01/myFirstBlazorApp`

Check out the following video to see the code in action:

`http://bit.ly/2Ro30VU`

What is Blazor?

Blazor is an open source .NET web framework that allows us to create client-side applications using C#/Razor and HTML. Web applications, created using Blazor, can run in the browser with the help of WebAssembly.

Razor is a markup syntax for C# and HTML. The name "Blazor" comes from the ability of the framework to run C#/Razor in the browser. Combining **browser** and **Razor** gives us the name **Blazor**.

Blazor provides a full stack .NET development experience by allowing us to use .NET throughout our application. We can create both the server and client side of the application using the same language, such as C#. It also allows us to share the common model class across the client and server.

 At the time of writing, Blazor is not yet a committed project. Microsoft defines it as an experimental project. Hence, it is not advisable to use Blazor for any production-ready applications.

What is WebAssembly?

WebAssembly (sometimes abbreviated as *Wasm*) is a low-level assembly-like language, which has a compact-binary format, and can run on all modern web browsers. It is suitable for compilation on the web because it is portable and has an efficient size and load time. It cannot be read or written by humans, as it is in low-level binary format. However, we can compile the code from other high-level languages, such as C#, in WebAssembly to facilitate their execution on the browser. WebAssembly is a subset of JavaScript, and is designed to run alongside JavaScript. It enables us to run code written in high-level languages on the browser at the native speed. WebAssembly runs .NET binaries on the browser using Mono. Mono is an open source .NET runtime, which is based on ECMA standards for C# and the **Common Language Runtime (CLR)**. Mono is sponsored by Microsoft, and allows us to create cross-platform apps using .NET. While executing a Blazor application, the Mono runtime gets compiled to WebAssembly on the browser.

WebAssembly is an open web standard and is supported on all major web browsers.

How does Blazor run in the browser?

Blazor executes on the browser with the help of WebAssembly. When we build and run a Blazor application, the following sequence of events take place:

1. The C#/Razor code files are compiled into .NET assemblies.
2. The browser downloads the `blazor.webassembly.js` file.
3. The `blazor-boot.json` file is downloaded to the browser. This file contains the application entry point and the reference to all the .NET assemblies that will be loaded by the browser.
4. The Mono .NET runtime is downloaded in the browser.
5. Blazor uses the Mono JavaScript library, `mono.js`, to bootstrap the `mono.wasm` Mono runtime in WebAssembly.
6. At the end, `mono.wasm` downloads, using the browser, the dynamic link libraries (DLLs) for the application and the .NET framework.

We will see all of these steps in action in the latter part of this chapter.

Why should we use Blazor?

Blazor provides us with many benefits over other client-side frameworks. The main advantages of Blazor are as follows:

- It allows us to have a full stack .NET development experience.
- We do not need to create separate model classes for client and server. Blazor allows us to reuse the same model class by sharing it with both client and server.
- We can use existing .NET APIs and tools to create rich web applications.
- It allows us to use the modern and feature-rich language of C#, which makes development easier.
- If you are already on a .NET platform, then the learning curve for Blazor is almost flat, as the only requirement to get started with it is an understanding of the C# language.
- Blazor is supported on both Visual Studio 2017 and Visual Studio Code. This provides a great .NET development experience across multiple platforms, including Linux, Windows, and Mac.
- It is an open source framework with great community support.

Features of Blazor

Blazor is inspired by modern UI frameworks such as Angular, React, and Vue. It supports all the necessary features to facilitate the development of SPAs. The SPA features supported by Blazor are as follows:

- **Component based architecture**: Blazor provides us with a component based architecture to create rich and composable UI.
- **Dependency injection**: This allows us to use services by injecting them into components.
- **Layouts**: We can share common UI elements (for example, menus) across pages using the layouts feature.
- **Routing**: We can redirect the client request from one component to another with the help of routing.
- **JavaScript interop**: This allows us to invoke a C# method from JavaScript, and we can call a JavaScript function or API from C# code.
- **Reload on build**: During development of the application, the application page reloads in the browser as we build it.

- **Forms and validation**: We can create interactive forms to handle user inputs, and apply validation techniques to handle any errors in the form. As of Blazor 0.6.0, inbuilt client-side validation support is not available, but the Blazor team has promised to provide it in a future release.
- We can also host the Blazor application on IIS and Azure Cloud.

Creating our first Blazor application

Since we have a basic understanding of Blazor, let's now create a sample Blazor application to get some in-depth knowledge.

We will use the CLI to create our Blazor application, and Visual Studio Code to explore the solution file. I am using a 64-bit Windows 10 machine.

Prerequisites

We need to make sure that the following two criteria are fulfilled before we start to create our Blazor application:

- Install the .NET Core SDK (version 2.1 or above) from `https://www.microsoft.com/net/download`.
- Download and install Visual Studio Code from `https://code.visualstudio.com/download`.

Steps to create the Blazor application

To create our first Blazor application, follow these steps:

1. Open to the folder where you want to create the Blazor application.
2. Press and hold *Shift,* and then right-click. This will open a menu with the option to **Open command window here**. Click on it to open Command Prompt in the current folder.

 If you have configured Windows Powershell on your machine, then you will get the option to **Open PowerShell window here**. You can use Windows PowerShell instead of Command Prompt.

3. Run the following command to install the Blazor templates on your machine. This is a one-time activity—you do not need to run this command the next time you create a *Blazor* app:

```
dotnet new -i Microsoft.AspNetCore.Blazor.Templates
```

Typing this command will install the templates, as shown in the following screenshot:

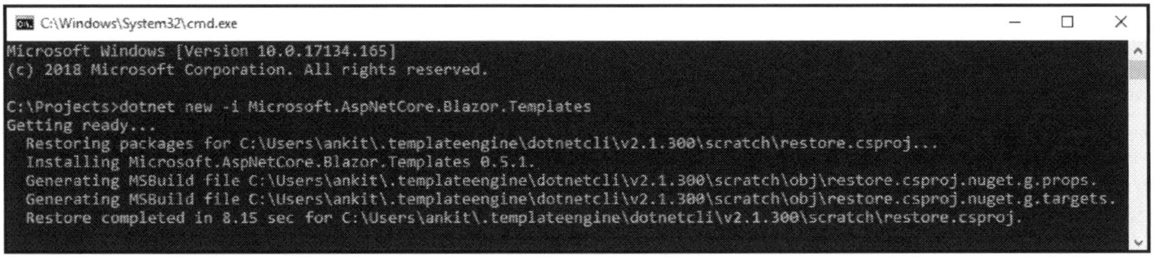

4. To create the Blazor application, run the following command:

```
dotnet new blazor -o myFirstBlazorApp
```

This will create a Blazor application with the name myFirstBlazorApp. Refer to the following screenshot:

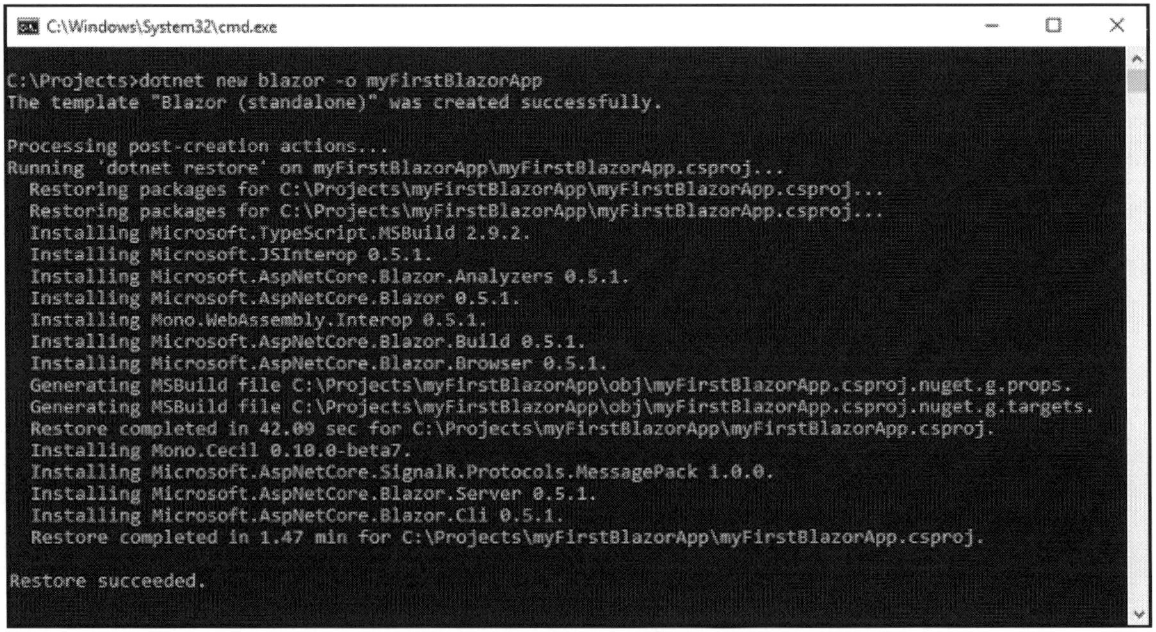

Once the solution file is created, open it using Visual Studio Code. You can see the folder structure of the application, as shown in the following screenshot:

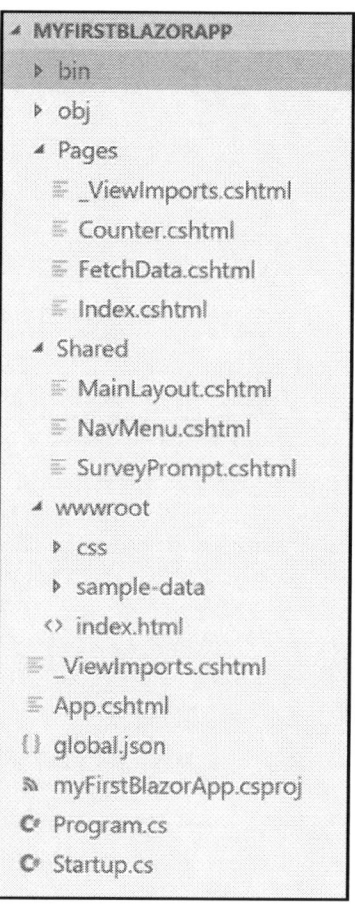

This is a default project template provided by the Blazor framework. Let's examine this project in detail.

The **Pages** folder has all of our **View** files, with the `.cshtml` extension. By default, we have the following four **View** files in this project:

- `_ViewImports.cshtml`: This file will import the MainLayout of our Blazor application. We will look at layouts in detail in `Chapter 2`, *Exploring Blazor Concepts.*

- `Counter.cshtml`: This page has the following code in it:

```
@page "/counter"

<h1>Counter</h1>

<p>Current count: @currentCount</p>

<button class="btn btn-primary" onclick="@IncrementCount">Click me</button>

@functions {
int currentCount = 0;

void IncrementCount()
{
currentCount++;
}
}
```

At the top of this snippet, we defined the route for this page using the `@page` directive. This means that, if we append `/page` to the root URL of the application, we will be redirected to this page. We will explore the Blazor routing in detail in Chapter 2, *Exploring Blazor Concepts*.

The HTML section contains a button that calls the `IncrementCount` method on click. The `IncrementCount` method is defined in the `@functions` section, and increases the value of a `currentCount` integer variable every time it is invoked.

The value of the `CurrentCount` variable is displayed using a `<p>` tag on the UI.

- `FetchData.cshtml`: This page demonstrates how to fetch data from a JSON file using a Web API. Consider the following code:

```
@page "/fetchdata"
@inject HttpClient Http

<h1>Weather forecast</h1>

<p>This component demonstrates fetching data from the server.</p>

@if (forecasts == null)
{
    <p><em>Loading...</em></p>
}
else
{
    <table class="table">
```

```
            <thead>
                <tr>
                    <th>Date</th>
                    <th>Temp. (C)</th>
                    <th>Temp. (F)</th>
                    <th>Summary</th>
                </tr>
            </thead>
            <tbody>
                @foreach (var forecast in forecasts)
                {
                    <tr>
                        <td>@forecast.Date.ToShortDateString()</td>
                        <td>@forecast.TemperatureC</td>
                        <td>@forecast.TemperatureF</td>
                        <td>@forecast.Summary</td>
                    </tr>
                }
            </tbody>
        </table>
}

@functions {
    WeatherForecast[] forecasts;

    protected override async Task OnInitAsync()
    {
        forecasts = await Http.GetJsonAsync<WeatherForecast[]>("sample-
data/weather.json");
    }

    class WeatherForecast
    {
        public DateTime Date { get; set; }
        public int TemperatureC { get; set; }
        public int TemperatureF { get; set; }
        public string Summary { get; set; }
    }
}
```

Apart from declaring the route for this page as /fetchdata, in the preceding snippet, we also injected an HttpClient service via dependency injection to facilitate a Web API call over HTTP.

Inside the @functions section, we defined a WeatherForecast class and created an array variable, forecasts, of the WeatherForecast type to hold the weather forecast data returned from the Web API call. The value of forecasts is bound to an HTML table using a foreach loop.

We get our data over HTTP inside the OnInitAsync method. This method is called when the FetchData component is initialized, which ensures that the data is populated on the UI as the web page finishes loading.

- Index.cshtml: This page contains some static content and is the first page to be displayed on the browser.

The Shared folder contains the pages that are shared across all the components. It contains the following three pages:

- MainLayout.cshtml: This will set up the main layout of our application
- NavMenu.cshtml: This will render a navigation menu on the left-hand side of our application
- SurveyPrompt.cshtml: This will ask the user to provide feedback of Blazor

Inside the wwwroot folder, the index.html file is present. Blazor requires blazor.webassembly.js to bootstrap. This JavaScript file is present in the \bin\Debug\netstandard2.0\dist_framework folder, and the <script> tag to include it in the project can be found in the wwwroot/index.html file.

This file contains the following code snippet:

```
<!DOCTYPE html>
<html>
<head>
    <meta charset="utf-8" />
    <meta name="viewport" content="width=device-width">
    <title>myFirstBlazorApp</title>
    <base href="/" />
    <link href="css/bootstrap/bootstrap.min.css" rel="stylesheet" />
    <link href="css/site.css" rel="stylesheet" />
</head>
<body>
    <app>Loading...</app>

    <script src="_framework/blazor.webassembly.js"></script>
</body>
</html>
```

The `Program.cs` and `Startup.cs` files have the code necessary to bootstrap the Blazor application. We will learn about them in the next section.

Understanding the Blazor boot process

So how does all of this boot up and run in the browser?

The entry point for our application is the `Main` method, which is defined in the `Program.cs` file. The `Program.cs` file contains the following code:

```
using Microsoft.AspNetCore.Blazor.Hosting;

namespace myFirstBlazorApp
{
    public class Program
    {
        public static void Main(string[] args)
        {
            CreateHostBuilder(args).Build().Run();
        }

        public static IWebAssemblyHostBuilder CreateHostBuilder(string[]
args) =>
            BlazorWebAssemblyHost.CreateDefaultBuilder()
                .UseBlazorStartup<Startup>();
    }
}
```

The `Main` method will invoke the `CreateHostBuilder` method, which will then call the `UseBlazorStartup` method and pass the `Startup` class as the argument. `UseBlazorStartup` is defined in the application metadata and is used to configure the `Microsoft.AspNetCore.Blazor.Hosting.IWebAssemblyHostBuilder` interface (an abstraction for configuring a Blazor browser-based application) to use the provided `Startup` class.

The `Startup` class is defined in `Startup.cs` using the following code snippet:

```
using Microsoft.AspNetCore.Blazor.Builder;
using Microsoft.Extensions.DependencyInjection;

namespace myFirstBlazorApp
{
    public class Startup
    {
```

```
public void ConfigureServices(IServiceCollection services)
{
}

public void Configure(IBlazorApplicationBuilder app)
{
    app.AddComponent<App>("app");
}
}
}
```

The `Configure` method of the `Startup` class will call the `AddComponent` method, and provides the <app> DOM selector, defined in `index.html`, as a parameter. The `AddComponent` method will associate the component type with the application, causing it to be displayed in the specified DOM element. Hence, the first element (the root component) to be displayed on the browser will be <app>. Then, the `blazor.webassembly.js` file is loaded on the browser that will handle the Mono runtime, and load the DLLs for the .NET framework and application.

HTML generation by Blazor

So far, we have learned how the Blazor application boots up. The next obvious question that comes to mind is, how is the HTML output generated and displayed on the browser?

Blazor uses the browser's DOM to generate web pages. But C# cannot access the DOM elements directly. Therefore, Blazor uses JavaScript's interop to access the DOM and manipulate the DOM elements, such as divs, buttons, textboxes, and so on.

The following flow diagram explains the process of DOM access by C#:

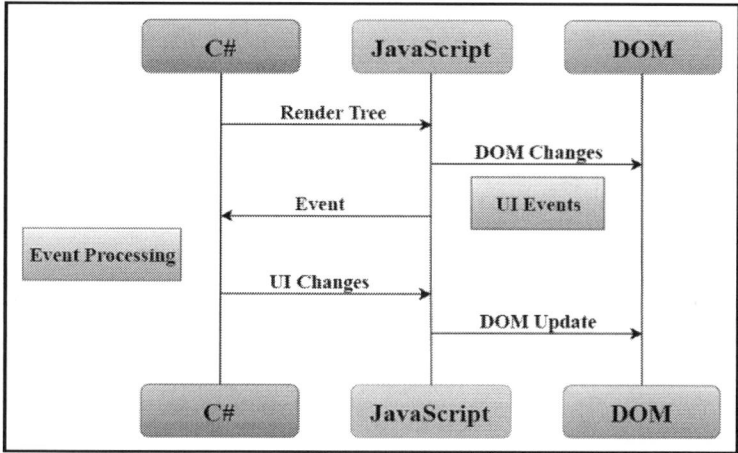

The process works as follows:

1. The C# code generates a render tree. A render tree is a hierarchical structure of UI components defined in our View page (the CSHTML page).

2. The render tree is then passed on to the JavaScript part of Blazor. The JavaScript code will then change the DOM contents according to the structure of the render tree.

3. Whenever the user interacts with the UI using a mouse click or key press, it creates an event. The JavaScript code listens to the user-generated event, and then internally invokes the `BrowserRendererEventDispatcher` class to dispatch the event to C#.

4. The event is then processed by the C# code, which makes any necessary changes as required.

5. These changes made by the C# code then need to be transferred to the UI. So, the JavaScript part of Blazor analyzes the render tree once again, and proceeds to apply only the UI changes (not the whole UI) to the DOM.

How Blazor generates render trees

So far, we have learned that render trees play a crucial role in HTML generation for our application. But how is the render tree generated in the first place? The answer to this question is that it's generated from the Razor code when the application is built. As you know, Razor is a template engine that runs on the server, and combines C# and HTML to generate dynamic web controls to be displayed on the web page. When the project is complied, the Razor engine generates the C# code from Razor code.

Let's say we have a Razor file with the name `xyz.cshtml`. When the application is built, a C# code file with the name `xyz.g.cs` is generated. This file has a `BuildRenderTree` method that creates the render tree from our UI elements.

Let's build our solution to get a better understanding of render trees.

Open the project solution folder using Visual Studio Code. Navigate to **View** | **Integrated Terminal** to open the Visual Studio Code terminal window.

 You can also use the keyboard shortcut *Ctrl* + ` to open the Visual Studio Code terminal window.

Run the following command to build the application:

```
dotnet build
```

Once the build is successful, it will generate files with the `g.cs` file extension in the `\obj\Debug\netstandard2.0\Pages` folder, corresponding to all our View files in the **Pages** folder. Navigate to `\obj\Debug\netstandard2.0\Pages` and open `Counter.g.cs`. It should contain the following code:

```
#pragma checksum "C:\BlazorProjects\myFirstBlazorApp\Pages\Counter.cshtml"
"{ff1816ec-aa5e-4d10-87f7-6f4963833460}"
"d4fabfd6e6d002e957b53fad126e1419708789b9"
#pragma warning disable 1591
namespace myFirstBlazorApp.Pages
{
    #line hidden
    using System;
    using System.Collections.Generic;
    using System.Linq;
    using System.Threading.Tasks;
    using Microsoft.AspNetCore.Blazor;
    using Microsoft.AspNetCore.Blazor.Components;
    using System.Net.Http;
    using Microsoft.AspNetCore.Blazor.Layouts;
    using Microsoft.AspNetCore.Blazor.Routing;
    using Microsoft.JSInterop;
    using myFirstBlazorApp;
    using myFirstBlazorApp.Shared;
[Microsoft.AspNetCore.Blazor.Layouts.LayoutAttribute(typeof(MainLayout))]

    [Microsoft.AspNetCore.Blazor.Components.RouteAttribute("/counter")]
    public class Counter :
```

```
Microsoft.AspNetCore.Blazor.Components.BlazorComponent
    {
        #pragma warning disable 1998
        protected override void
BuildRenderTree(Microsoft.AspNetCore.Blazor.RenderTree.RenderTreeBuilder
builder)
        {
            base.BuildRenderTree(builder);
            builder.OpenElement(0, "h1");
            builder.AddContent(1, "Counter");
            builder.CloseElement();
            builder.AddContent(2, "\n\n");
            builder.OpenElement(3, "p");
            builder.AddContent(4, "Current count: ");
            builder.AddContent(5, currentCount);
            builder.CloseElement();
            builder.AddContent(6, "\n\n");
            builder.OpenElement(7, "button");
            builder.AddAttribute(8, "class", "btn btn-primary");
            builder.AddAttribute(9, "onclick",
Microsoft.AspNetCore.Blazor.Components.BindMethods.GetEventHandlerValue<Mic
rosoft.AspNetCore.Blazor.UIMouseEventArgs>(IncrementCount));
            builder.AddContent(10, "Click me");
            builder.CloseElement();
        }
        #pragma warning restore 1998
#line 9 "C:\BlazorProjects\myFirstBlazorApp\Pages\Counter.cshtml"
    int currentCount = 0;

    void IncrementCount()
    {
        currentCount++;
    }

#line default
#line hidden
    }
}
#pragma warning restore 1591
```

The class defined in this file has the same name as our View file; that is, Counter. Inside the Counter class, we have overridden the BuildRenderTree method to create the render tree from our UI elements. You can also observe that the variables and methods defined in the @functions section of our View page are also defined here. All of these C# code files with the .G.CS extension are compiled to a .dll file at runtime, and then downloaded to the browser by mono.wasm.

After the successful build, a `blazor-boot.json` file is also created inside the `\obj\Debug\netstandard2.0\blazor` folder. This file contains the following code:

```
{
    "main": "myFirstBlazorApp.dll",
    "entryPoint": "myFirstBlazorApp.Program::Main",
    "assemblyReferences": [
        "Microsoft.AspNetCore.Blazor.Browser.dll",
        "Microsoft.AspNetCore.Blazor.dll",
        "Microsoft.Extensions.DependencyInjection.Abstractions.dll",
        "Microsoft.Extensions.DependencyInjection.dll",
        "Microsoft.JSInterop.dll",
        "Mono.WebAssembly.Interop.dll",
        "mscorlib.dll",
        "netstandard.dll",
        "System.Core.dll",
        "System.dll",
        "System.Net.Http.dll"
    ],
    "cssReferences": [],
    "jsReferences": [],
    "linkerEnabled": true
}
```

It contains the entry point of our application, and also the .NET assembly references that will be downloaded to the browser by `mono.wasm`.

Demo execution of a Blazor application

Now, we will run our application and see how it is rendered in the browser.

To start the Blazor app in the browser, follow these steps:

1. Navigate to **Integrated terminal** in Visual Studio Code.
2. Execute the following command:

dotnet run

3. You will observe that the application has started, and it will give you two URLs on which the app is listening. Refer to the following screenshot:

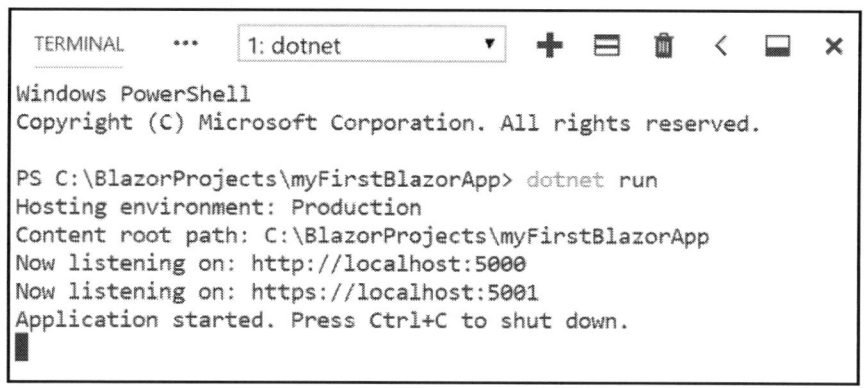

One URL is using the `http` protocol, while the other is using `https`. You need to open either of the URLs on which the application is listening. This can be done in any browser of your choice.

In this demo, I will open `https://localhost:5001/` in the Google Chrome browser. As the application is loading, open the Chrome developer tools. Navigate to the **Network** tab and you can see the Blazor application boot process as follows:

Name	Status	Type	Initiator	Size
localhost	200	document	Other	664 B
bootstrap.min.css	200	stylesheet	(index)	142 KB
site.css	200	stylesheet	(index)	2.4 KB
blazor.webassembly.js	200	script	(index)	38.1 KB
open-iconic-bootstrap.min.css	200	stylesheet	(index)	9.4 KB
blazor.boot.json	200	fetch	blazor.webassembly.js:1	728 B
mono.js	200	script	blazor.webassembly.js:1	175 KB
favicon.ico	200	text/html	Other	664 B
mono.wasm	200	fetch	mono.js:1	1.7 MB
myFirstBlazorApp.dll	200	xhr	blazor.webassembly.js:1	15.7 KB
Microsoft.AspNetCore.Blazor.Browser.dll	200	xhr	blazor.webassembly.js:1	38.1 KB
Microsoft.AspNetCore.Blazor.dll	200	xhr	blazor.webassembly.js:1	101 KB
Microsoft.Extensions.DependencyInjection.Abstractions.dll	200	xhr	blazor.webassembly.js:1	36.2 KB
Microsoft.Extensions.DependencyInjection.dll	200	xhr	blazor.webassembly.js:1	51.7 KB
Microsoft.JSInterop.dll	200	xhr	blazor.webassembly.js:1	50.6 KB
Mono.WebAssembly.Interop.dll	200	xhr	blazor.webassembly.js:1	16.6 KB
mscorlib.dll	200	xhr	blazor.webassembly.js:1	1.6 MB
netstandard.dll	200	xhr	blazor.webassembly.js:1	26.7 KB
System.Core.dll	200	xhr	blazor.webassembly.js:1	334 KB
System.dll	200	xhr	blazor.webassembly.js:1	87.2 KB

As we discussed earlier, you can see the Blazor execution process in action here. blazor.webassembly.js is the first file to be downloaded to the browser. Then, the browser loads the blazor-boot.json file and, after that, the mono.js .NET runtime is downloaded to the browser. After this, mono.wasm downloads the application's DLL file, myFirstBlazorApp.dll. The browser will then download all the assembly reference DLLs mentioned in the blazor-boot.json file.

The first page to be displayed on the browser will be the Home page. This is a very basic page, which displays a welcome message and a hyperlink to a survey about Blazor:

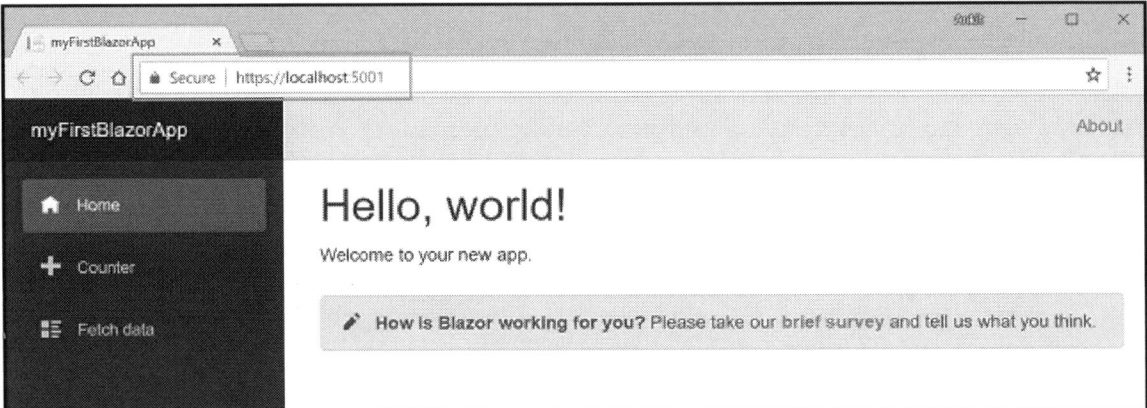

The left-hand side of the web page has a navigation menu, which contains links to the Home, Counter, and Fetch data pages. The navigation menu is a shared component, defined in the \Shared\NavMenu.cshtml file.

Click on **Counter** in the navigation menu. You will be redirected to the **Counter** page, as shown in the following screenshot:

Notice that the URL has /counter attached to it. This is the route of this page, as defined using the @page directive in the Counter.cshtml file. This page has a button that will increase the count when clicked. The counter value will be displayed onscreen as you press the button.

As shown in the following screenshot, I have clicked on the counter 4 times, so it displays **4** as a result:

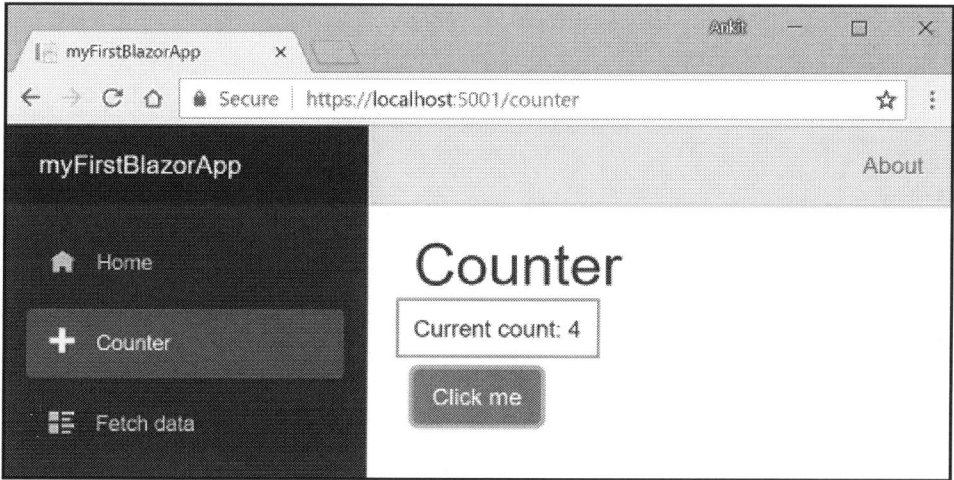

Click on **Fetch data** in the navigation menu. This will redirect you to the Weather forecast page. Notice that the URL of this page has /fetchdata attached to it as the route for this page:

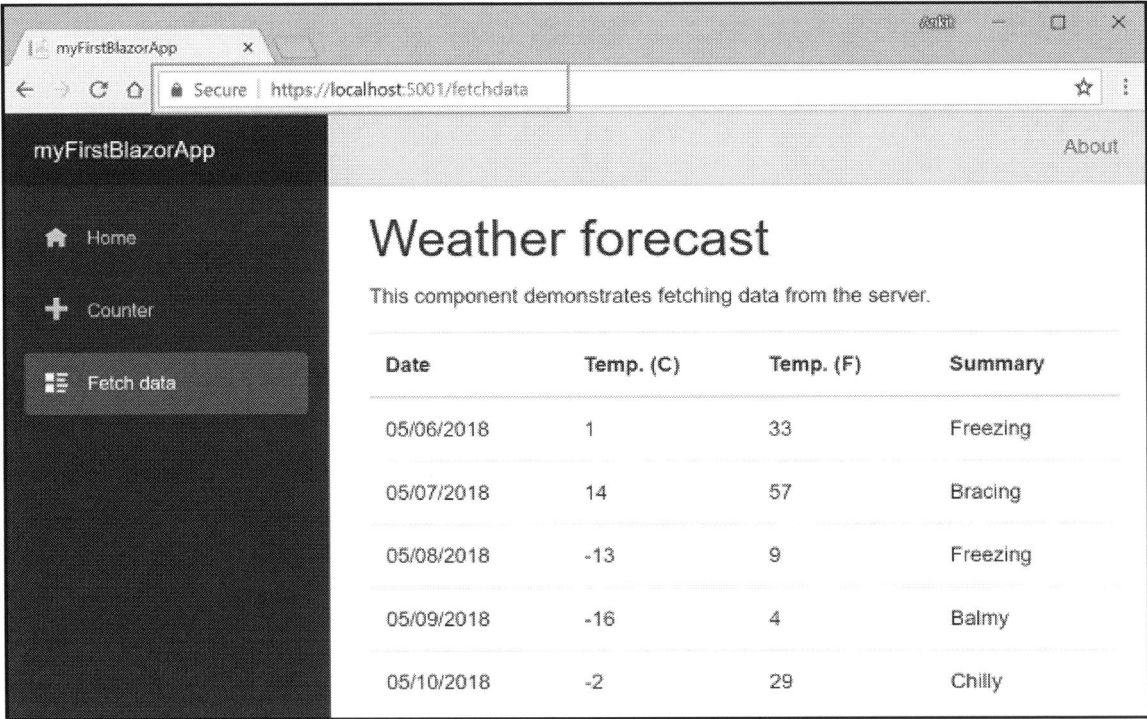

This page will display a set of static data in an HTML table. This data is fetched from the \wwwroot\sample-data\weather.json file and is bound to the table using a foreach loop.

Summary

In this chapter, we learned about the new .NET web framework, Blazor. Blazor allows us to create a client-side application using C#/Razor code. We now understand what Blazor is, and what its advantages are. We also learned about the execution model of the Blazor framework. We created a sample Blazor application using the CLI, and executed it to see our first Blazor app in action. Remember—Blazor is an experimental project with no official support from Microsoft. Hence, it is not advisable to use it for production applications.

In the next chapter, we will explore in detail some of the important concepts in Blazor, such as components, layouts, data binding, and so on.

Exploring Blazor Concepts 2

In the last chapter, we learned about the basics of Blazor. We saw how the Blazor framework provides us with the facility to write and execute C# code for a client-side application.

In this chapter, we will explore what I love to call the *building blocks* of the Blazor framework. The concepts that we will learn in this chapter will help us to understand how the Blazor framework is designed, and how it works as a framework.

We will explore the following topics in this chapter:

- Blazor components
- Data binding in Blazor
- Event handling with Blazor
- Life cycle methods of Blazor
- Layouts in Blazor
- How dependency injection works in Blazor
- Routing in Blazor
- How to render raw HTML on a web page

A good understanding of these concepts is essential to reap all of the benefits of Blazor, and will also help us to write better and cleaner code. We will learn all of these concepts with the help of a sample application. So, without further ado, let's get started.

Technical requirements

You need to have knowledge on following concepts:

- C#
- ASP.NET Core
- Entity Framework Core
- Ado.NET

You should also install following software to start Blazor development.

- .NET Core 2.1 or above SDK.
- Visual Studio Code
- Visual Studio 2017 v15.7 or above
- ASP.NET Core Blazor Language Services extension

The code files of this chapter can be found on GitHub:
```
https://github.com/PacktPublishing/Blazor-Quick-Start-Guide/tree/master/
Chapter02/BlazorDemo
```

Check out the following video to see the code in action:

```
http://bit.ly/2yFoeaW
```

Creating a sample Blazor application

We will learn about all of the concepts mentioned in the introduction to this chapter with the help of code samples, so we need to create a sample Blazor application to write and execute the code as we proceed.

We already discussed the steps that are required to create a Blazor application in the previous chapter. Follow the same steps to create a sample app, this time with the name `BlazorDemo`.

 Since you already installed the Blazor template on your machine in the first chapter, you can skip the first step there when creating your sample application.

Once the `BlazorDemo` project file has been created, open it using **Visual Studio (VS)** Code and build the application code by using the `dotnet build` command.

Components in Blazor

Blazor is a component-based framework. A Blazor component is defined as a block of the UI, consisting of both HTML and the corresponding business logic. The HTML helps to render the component on the web page, and the logic handles the database operations or the event handling. A Blazor component is lightweight, flexible, and shareable across different projects.

The bottom line is that all UI fragments can be termed **components** in Blazor.

Creating a component in Blazor

We will now discuss the following two methods for creating components in Blazor:

- Using a single file
- Using a code-behind file

Let's examine both of them in detail in this section.

Using a single file

We will use a single file with the `.cshtml` extension to create our component. To create a component file, right-click on the Pages folder of your BlazorDemo project and select **New File**. Type in the filename as `CompDemo.cshtml` and press *Enter* to create the file.

Put the following lines of code inside this file:

```
@page "/singlepagecomp"

<h1>@PageTitle</h1>
<hr/>
<p>This component is created using a single .cshtml page.</p>

@functions {
string PageTitle = "Component Demo";
}
```

Both the HTML and the @functions section are defined in only one file, that is, CompDemo.cshtml. Here, we have defined a PageTitle property to set the title on the page. On execution, this page will show a heading and a sample message, as defined in this property. But before running this application, we need to add the navigation link to this page to the \Shared\NavMenu.cshtml file. Open the \Shared\NavMenu.cshtml file and add the following code to it:

```
<li class="nav-item px-3">
  <NavLink class="nav-link" href="singlepagecomp">
    <span class="oi oi-list-rich" aria-hidden="true"></span> Comp Demo
  </NavLink>
</li>
```

This will add a Comp Demo navigation menu item, which will redirect to the CompDemo.cshtml page when clicked.

The execution is done in the same way as we discussed in the previous chapter. Type the dotnet run command into the VS Code console and press *Enter*. Open the URL in the browser, and you should see a page similar to one shown in the following screenshot:

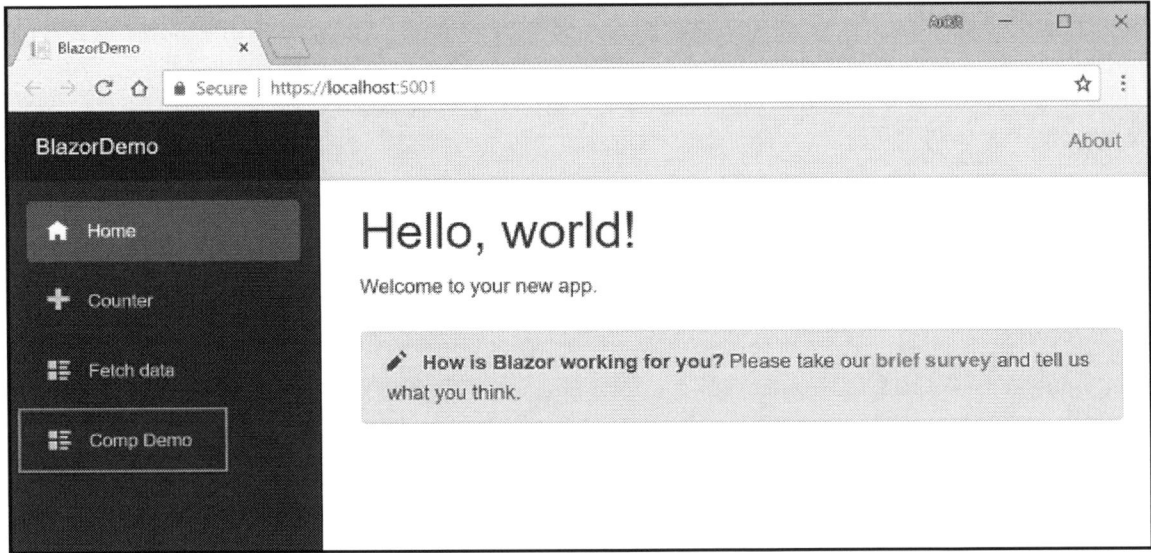

You can observe that we have a Comp Demo link in the navigation menu on the left. Click on it to navigate to the CompDemo.cshtml component. It should open a page like the one shown in the following screenshot:

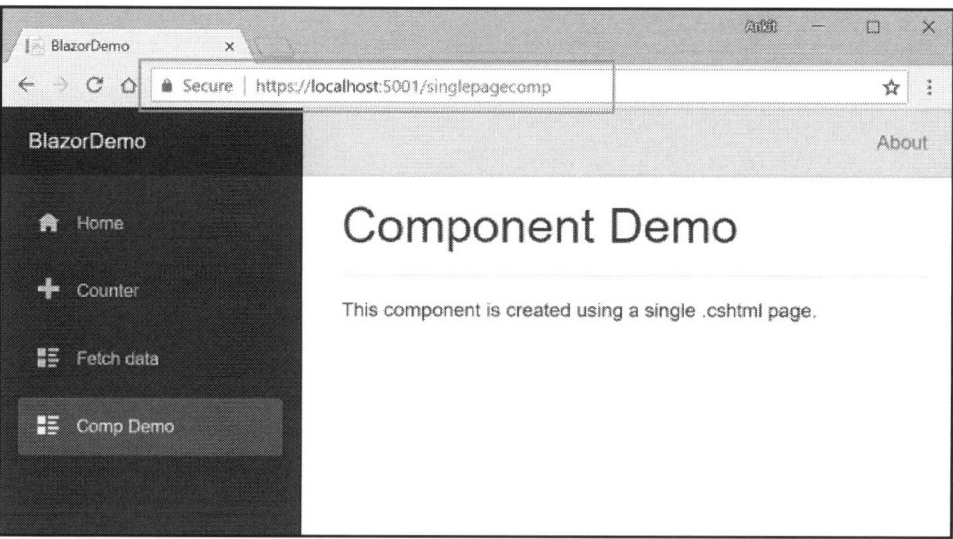

You can observe that the route URL of the page has /singlepagecomp attached to it, and that the message is being displayed on the page as we defined it in our component.

Using a code-behind file

In this method, we will be using two files to create our component—one file to hold the HTML part of the component, and another to hold the logic part of the component.

To add the files, we will follow the same process that we employed earlier. Right-click on the Pages folder and select New File. Name the file CodeBehindComp.cshtml and press *Enter* to create the file. This file will contain the HTML section of our component. Similarly, add one more file, CodeBehindComp.cshtml.cs, to the Pages folder. This file will contain our logic section, which will define the members of the component class.

Open CodeBehindComp.cshtml.cs and put the following code into it:

```
using Microsoft.AspNetCore.Blazor.Components;

namespace BlazorDemo.Pages
{
    public class CodeBehindCompModel : BlazorComponent
    {
        public string PageTitle { get; set; } = "Component Demo";
    }
}
```

Here, we have defined a `CodeBehindCompModel` class that contains a `PageTitle` string property, which sets the title of the component once it is rendered as a web page in the browser.

 The Blazor compiler generates classes for all of the view pages with the same name as the page name; hence, we have suffixed the class name with the word "model" to distinguish it from the page name. If we use the same class name as page name (CodeBehindComp, in this case), then it will result in a compile time error.

Open `CodeBehindComp.cshtml` and put the following code into it:

```
@page "/codebehindcomp"
@inherits CodeBehindCompModel

<h1>@PageTitle</h1>

<p>This component is created using two files,.cshtml and.cshtml.cs</p>
```

This page will inherit the class defined in our code-behind page by using the `@inherits` directive. This allows us to use all of the properties and methods defined in the class from this page.

Add the navigation link for this page, as defined in the following snippet, inside the `\Shared\NavMenu.cshtml` file:

```
<li class="nav-item px-3">
  <NavLink class="nav-link" href="codebehindcomp">
    <span class="oi oi-list-rich" aria-hidden="true"></span> Code Behind
Comp
  </NavLink>
</li>
```

Execute the application by running the `dotnet run` command, and click on the **Code Behind Comp** link in the navigation menu on the left. You should see a page similar to the one shown in the following screenshot:

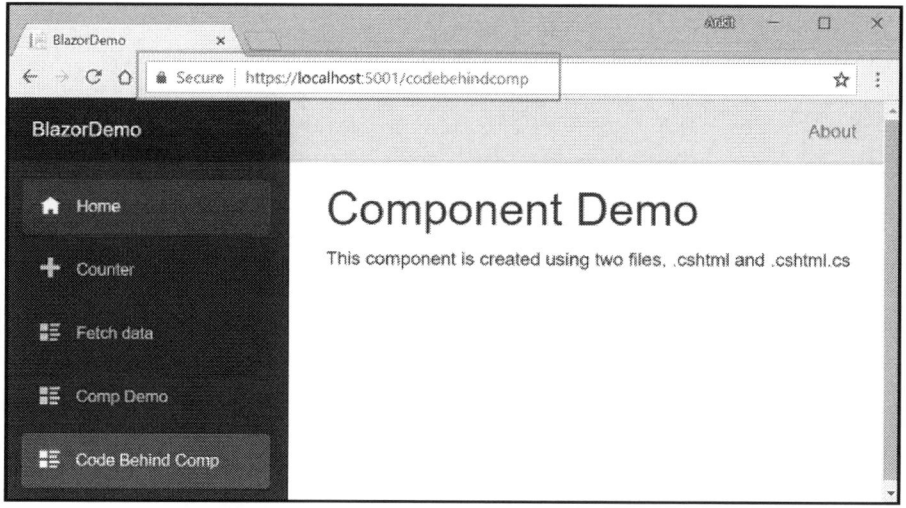

Here, the title of the page is set to **Component Demo** because of the PageTitle variable defined in the code-behind file, whereas the messages is displayed using the HTML defined in the `.cshtml` file.

Using a component within another component

The Blazor framework also allows us to use a component within another component. This will work like a parent-child relationship, where the parent component can refer to the child component.

We will demonstrate this concept with the help of an example.

Create two files in the Pages folder, and name them `ParentComp.cshtml` and `ChildComp.cshtml`.

Open the `ChildComp.cshtml` page and put the following code into it:

```
<hr/>
<h3> Welcome to the Child Component</h3>

<div>@ChildContent</div>

@functions {

[Parameter]
private RenderFragment ChildContent { get; set; }
}
```

Here, we first defined some dummy messages to be displayed on the page. There is no route defined for this component, as it will act as a child component and will be referred to by another component. The parent component will pass the content to the child component so that it can be rendered in a `<div>` tag. We will use a `RenderFragment` property, `ChildContent`, to hold the message supplied by the parent component. `ChildContent` is a component parameter decorated by the `[Parameter]` attribute. `RenderFragment` is defined in the application metadata, and represents a segment of the UI content, implemented as a delegate that writes the content to an instance of `Microsoft.AspNetCore.Blazor.RenderTree.RenderTreeBuilder`.

The component parameter must fulfill the following two criteria:

- It must be a non-public property
- The component parameter that will receive the `RenderFragment` content must be named `ChildContent`

Open `ParentComp.cshtml` and enter the following code:

```
@page "/ParentComponent"

<h1>Parent-child example</h1>

<ChildComp>
    This is parent component data.
</ChildComp>
```

We defined the route of this application at the top of the preceding snippet as `/ParentComponent`. To refer to the child component, we use a tag with the same name as the file name of the child component, which is `<ChildComp>` in this case. The `RenderFragment` parameter is provided between the tags of the child component. In this case, we provide a string message that will be rendered by the child component.

Before executing the code, we need to add the following navigation link of the parent component to the `\Shared\NavMenu.cshtml` file:

```
<li class="nav-item px-3">
  <NavLink class="nav-link" href="ParentComponent">
    <span class="oi oi-list-rich" aria-hidden="true"></span> Parent-Child
  </NavLink>
</li>
```

Run the application and click on the **Parent-Child** link in the navigation menu. You should see a page similar to the following screenshot:

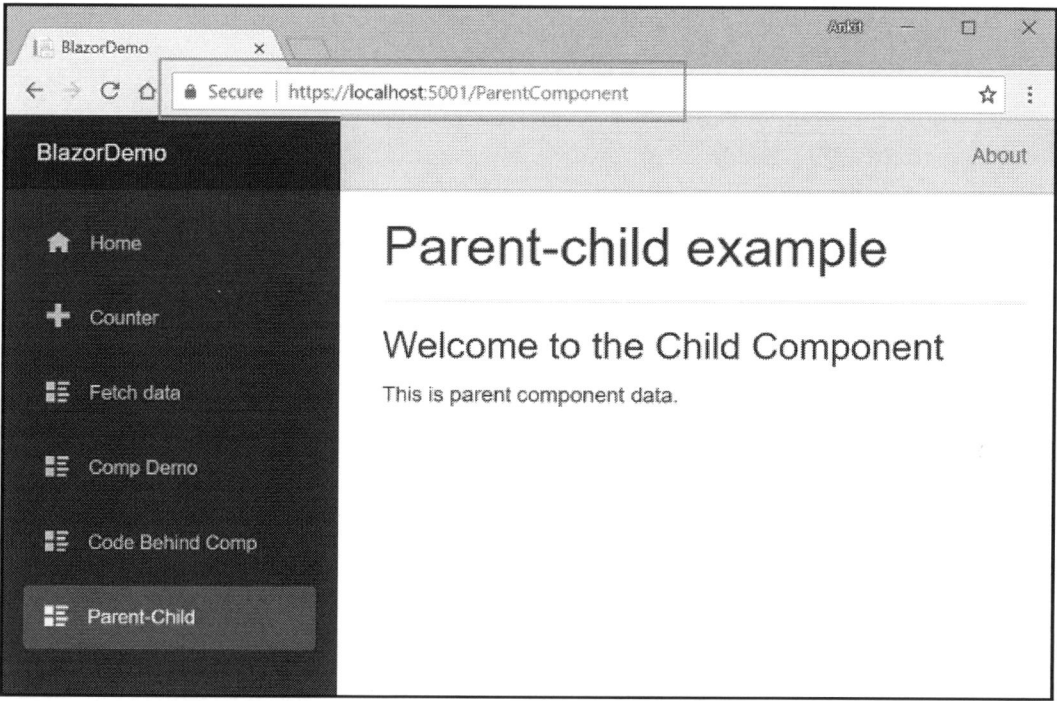

You can see the content of the parent component, along with that of the child component, displayed on the page.

Data binding in Blazor

Data binding is one of the most important features of any framework. Blazor also provides data binding capabilities. In this section, we will explore the following two techniques of data binding in Blazor:

- One-way data binding
- Two-way data binding

One-way data binding

One-way data binding allows us to bind the value of a property or variable to HTML DOM elements, but not vice versa. To bind a property to an HTML tag, we need to pass the property name, prefixed with the @ symbol.

We will examine this with the help of an example. Create a file, `DataBinding.cshtml`, in the Pages folder and put the following code into it:

```
@page "/databinding"

<h1>Data Binding example</h1>
<hr />

<h3>One way data binding</h3>
<p>@oneWayData</p>
@functions{
    string oneWayData = "This is a sample string";
}
```

In the preceding snippet, we defined and initialized a `oneWayData` string variable. This variable is used to populate the <p> tag by binding to it, via @oneWayData.

Two-way data binding

Two-way data binding allows us to bind the value of a property or variable to HTML DOM elements, and vice versa. We can achieve two-way data binding by using the `bind` attribute.

Update the `DataBinding.cshtml` file with the following code:

```
@page "/databinding"

<h1>Data Binding example</h1>
<hr />

<h3>One way data binding</h3>
<p>@oneWayData</p>

<hr />

<h3>Two way data binding</h3>
Enter your Age: <input type="text" bind=@age /><br />
<p>You are @age years old.</p>
```

```
@functions{
    string oneWayData = "This is a sample string";

    int age { get; set; }
}
```

In the preceding snippet, we defined an integer property called `age`. It binds to the `<input/>` field using the syntax `bind=@age`. The `Age` property then simultaneously binds to the `<p>` tag to display the value entered into the input field.

Add the navigation link for `DataBinding.cshtml` in to the `\Shared\NavMenu.cshtml` file by using the following code:

```
<li class="nav-item px-3">
  <NavLink class="nav-link" href="databinding">
    <span class="oi oi-list-rich" aria-hidden="true"></span> Data-binding
  </NavLink>
</li>
```

Execute the application, and click on **Data-binding** in the navigation menu. You should see a page similar to the one shown in the following screenshot:

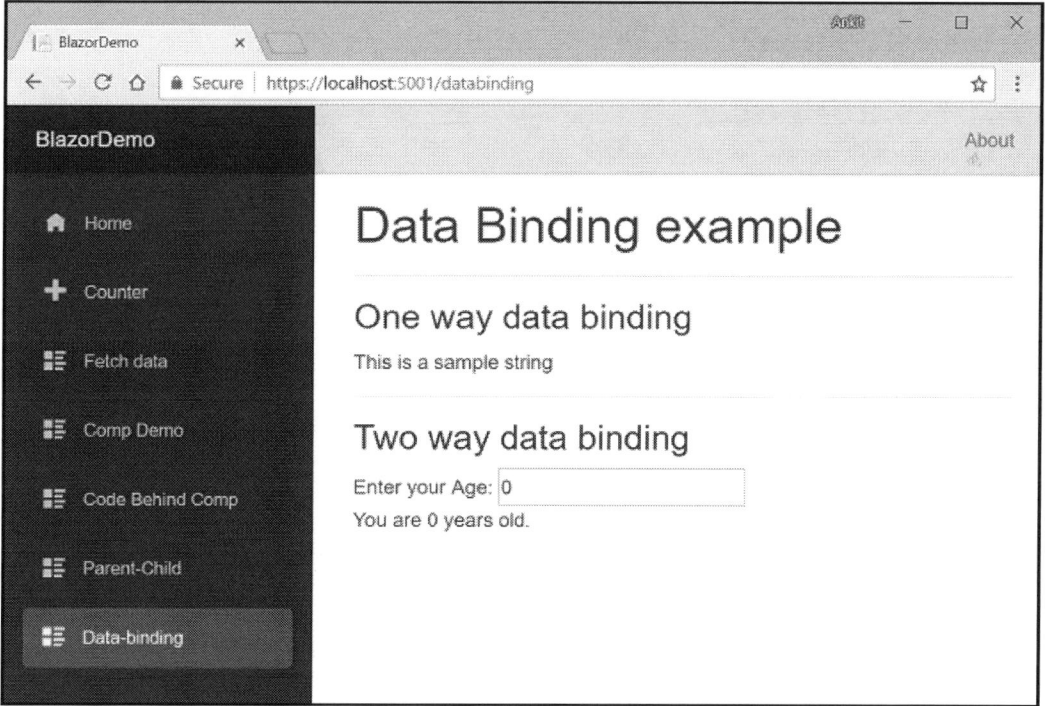

The one-way data binding section will display the static message that we set in the value of the `oneWayData` variable, whereas the two-way data binding section will display an input box asking for you to enter your age. Enter any numeric value, and you should observe that the message beneath the input box is also updated, as shown in the following screenshot:

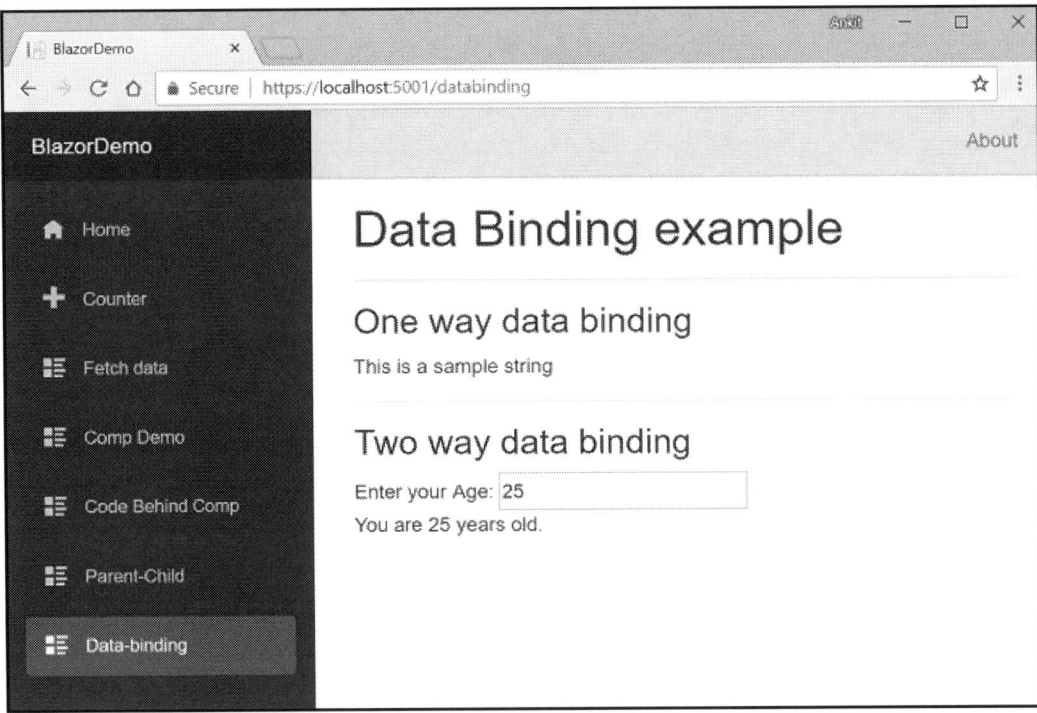

We can also bind to a formatted string. At the time of writing this book , Blazor allows us to bind to `DateTime` format strings only. Take a look at the following example:

```
Today's Date is: <input bind="@TodayDate" format-value="yyyy-MM-dd" />

@functions{
    private DateTime TodayDate { get; set; } = DateTime.Now;
}
```

The `format-value` attribute is used to specify the date format that we need to bind. It will give you an output similar to one shown in the following screenshot. Here, I show just the portion of the page that displays this input field:

Event handling with Blazor

Blazor also provides us with event handling support. At the time of writing this book, Blazor supports the following four types of event handling:

- UI click event
- UI change event
- UI keyboard event
- UI mouse event

Let's examine this with the help of an example. Add a new file to the `Pages` folder and name it `EventHandeling.cshtml`. Put the following code inside the file:

```
@page "/eventhandeling"

<h1>Event Handeling example</h1>
<hr />

<div>
    <button class="btn" onclick="@ButtonClicked">
        Click me
    </button>
</div>
<br />
<select class="form-control col-md-4" onchange="@SelectGender">
    <option value="">-- Select Gender --</option>
    <option value="Male">Male</option>
    <option value="Female">Female</option>
</select>
<br />
<p>Selected Gender : @Gender </p>

@functions{

    string Gender { get; set; }
```

```
    void ButtonClicked(UIMouseEventArgs e)
    {
        Console.WriteLine("button clicked");
    }

    void SelectGender(UIChangeEventArgs e)
    {
        Gender = e.Value.ToString();
    }
}
```

We will invoke the `onclick` event of the **Click Me** button, which, when the button is clicked, will call the `ButtonClicked` method. In a normal scenario, a button-click event is triggered to handle any input data, form submission, and so on. However, for this sample code, we will just print an output to the console of the developer's tool in the browser.

We have also defined a drop-down list to select the gender value. The `Onchange` event of the drop-down list will call the `SelectGender` method to set the value of the `Gender` property to the selected item, and will then bind it to a <p> tag to be displayed on the UI.

Add the navigation link to this page in the `NavMenu.cshtml` file by using the same technique discussed in the previous section. Launch the application and navigate to this page. Click on the button, and it will display the message on the console. This shows that our `onclick` event is indeed firing on button-click. Again, by selecting any value from the drop-down list, the <p> tag should be updated to show that our `onchange` event is firing on the selection of a value from the drop-down list. Refer to the following screenshot for the sample output:

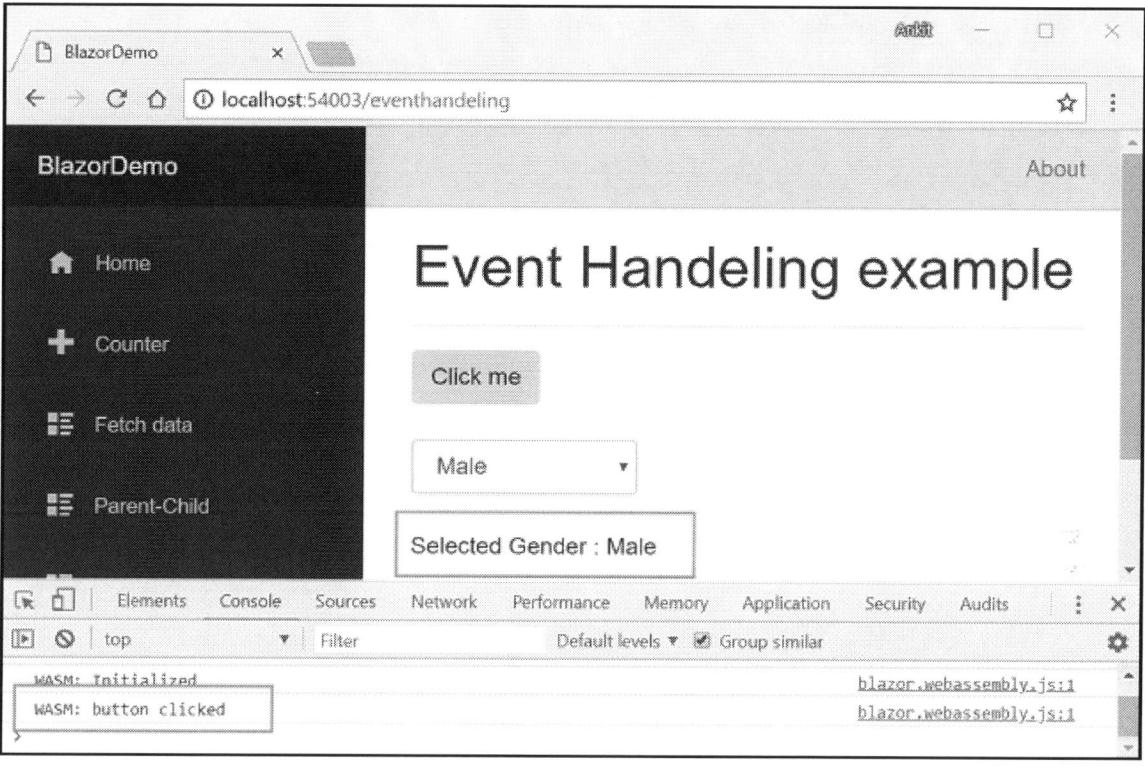

Life cycle methods of Blazor

Blazor provides us with eight life cycle methods. It has both synchronous, as well as asynchronous, methods. Let's examine all of them with the help of some sample code:

- OnInit: This method executes the code after the component has been initialized. This method is a synchronous method, and is generally used to call the APIs to load the data. The method signature is as follows:

```
protected override void OnInit()
{
  // Some method call to load data
}
```

- `OnInitAsync`: This is the asynchronous version of the `OnInit` method. Similar to `OnInit`, it is also called after the component has been initialized. To invoke the API methods using `OnInit`, we need to use the await keyword. The method signature is as follows:

```
protected override async Task OnInitAsync()
{
    await someMethod();
}
```

- `OnParametersSet`: As the name suggests, this method is called when the parameters are set; that is, after a component is received, the parameters from the parent component assign the values to their corresponding properties. This is a synchronous method, and the method signature is as follows:

```
protected override void OnParametersSet()
{
    // Some method call
}
```

- `OnParametersSetAsync`: This is the asynchronous version of the `OnParametersSet` method. To make any method call inside this, we need to use the await keyword. Both `OnParametersSet` and `OnParametersSetAsync` are invoked after the execution of the `OnInit` method during component initialization. The method signature of `OnParametersSetAsync` is as follows:

```
protected override async Task OnParametersSetAsync()
{
  await someMethod();
}
```

- `OnAfterRender`: This method is called after the component has finished rendering. We can use this method to perform any extra steps required for component initialization, such as activating any third-party JavaScript libraries that use the rendered DOM elements. This is a synchronous method and the method signature is as follows:

```
protected override void OnAfterRender()
{
  // Some method call
}
```

- OnAfterRenderAsync: This is the asynchronous version of the OnAfterRender method. As with other asynchronous methods, it also requires the await keyword to make any external method calls. The method signature is as follows:

```
protected override async Task OnAfterRenderAsync()
{
  await someMethod();
}
```

- SetParameters: If we want to execute some code before setting the parameters, we can use this method. The method signature is as follows:

```
public override void SetParameters(ParameterCollection parameters)
{
  // custom code

  base.SetParameters(parameters);
}
```

You can use your custom method to manipulate the incoming parameters in any way required before invoking the base.SetParameters method.

- ShouldRender: This is used to suppress the refreshing of UI. If we return true from this method, then the UI is refreshed; otherwise, it will not be refreshed. However, it always performs the initial rendering of the component. The method signature is as follows:

```
protected override bool ShouldRender()
{
  bool condition = someMethod();

  if (condition)
  {
    return true;
  }
  else
  {
    return false;
  }
}
```

Layouts in Blazor

In a multiple page application, some parts of the pages remain the same throughout the application, such as menus, headers, footers, and so on. However, we cannot write code for the common part in all the pages. Therefore, to solve this issue in Blazor, we use layouts. A layout is a Blazor component that contains Razor or C# code, and is used to handle the UI features that are common across multiple components.

A layout component must fulfill the following two criteria:

- It should inherit from the BlazorLayoutComponent class. This class defines a Body property, which contains the content that needs to be rendered inside the layout.
- It must define a location to specify where the body content has to be rendered. This is done by using some Razor syntax in the form of @Body. At the time of page rendering, @Body is replaced by the content of the layout.

The default template of Blazor provides us with a layout by default. Open the \BlazorDemo\Shared\MainLayout.cshtml file and you should see the following code inside it:

```
@inherits BlazorLayoutComponent

<div class="sidebar">
    <NavMenu />
</div>

<div class="main">
    <div class="top-row px-4">
        <a href="http://blazor.net" target="_blank" class="ml-md-
auto">About</a>
    </div>

    <div class="content px-4">
        @Body
    </div>
</div>
```

Note that it inherits the BlazorLayoutComponent class at the top of the preceding snippet, and later defines a @Body section to render the page component.

To use a layout inside our component, we need to refer to it by using the `@layout` directive. Take a look at the following sample code:

```
@layout MainLayout
@page "/demo"

<h1>This is a demo page</h1>
```

At runtime, the `@Body` property in the `MainLayout` is replaced by the contents of this page.

This method of referring to a layout is simple to use, but if we have a lot of pages, then it becomes impractical to use `@layout MainLayout` in all the pages. So, to alleviate this situation, we need to refer to our layout in a centralized location, from which other pages can take the reference.

The Pages folder of a Blazor application contains a template file, named `_ViewImports.cshtml`. We need to include the reference to our layout in this file. The compiler will make sure that it applies the directives specified in the `_ViewImports.cshtml` file in all the Razor files in the same folder, and all of their subfolders. If you open the `\Pages\_ViewImports.cshtml` file, you can observe that it already has the reference to our MainLayout, thus ensuring that of all the existing and newly created pages have the same look and feel.

Blazor also supports nesting of layout pages. Nesting of the layout means that we can refer to a layout, which in turn will refer to another layout. Take a look at the following code samples to understand how layout nesting is done in Blazor.

We will create a `DemoComponent.cshtml` file with the following code:

```
@layout ChildLayout

<h1>This is a demo page</h1>
```

This page is referring to `ChildLayout`. We will define the `ChildLayout.cshmtl` page in the `Shared` folder. We will use the following code:

```
@layout MainLayout
@inherits BlazorLayoutComponent

@* Some code for layout structure *@

@Body
```

This layout reference is our MainLayout, which is already defined in the shared folder. When we execute the application, the `DemoComponent.cshtml` page will render the content of both `ChildLayout` and `MainLayout`.

Dependency injection in Blazor

Dependency injection is a software design pattern where one object provides its dependency to another object. This allows us to share a single instance of a service class across multiple components. Blazor provides us with built-in dependency injection support, based on the ASP.NET Core DI system.

Dependency injection in Blazor allows us to provide the service instances to our components. We can configure the dependency injection service in the `ConfigureServices` method of the `Startup` class, inside the `Startup.cs` file. The `ConfigureServices` method is supplied an instance of `IServiceCollection`, which specifies the contract for a collection of service descriptors.

Take a look at the following sample code snippet:

```
public void ConfigureServices(IServiceCollection services)
{
    services.AddSingleton<EmployeeService>();
}
```

Here, we inject a sample service, `EmployeeService`, in to our components. We can use the methods of this service by creating a reference variable to it inside our components.

We can configure the services that inside our `ConfigureServices` method in three different ways:

- **Singleton**: This creates a single instance of a service that is shared across all components. To add this type of service, we need to use the `services.AddSingleton <SERVICE_NAME>` extension method, as shown in the preceding example.
- **Transient**: This creates a new instance of a service every time a component requests this service. To add this type of service, we need to call the `services.AddTransient<SERVICE_NAME>` extension method.
- **Scoped**: This creates one instance of service per web request. At the time of writing this book, Blazor does not support the scope concept of dependency injection. To add this type of service, we need to call the `services.AddScoped<SERVICE_NAME>` extension method.

Blazor also provides two default services, that we can use directly in our component without having to configure them as such in the `Startup` class. These default services are `IUriHelper` and `HttpClient`.

Take a look at the following sample code to understand how these work:

```
@page "/demoapp"

@inject HttpClient Http
@inject Microsoft.AspNetCore.Blazor.Services.IUriHelper UriHelper

protected override async Task OnInitAsync()
{
   var obj = await Http.GetJsonAsync<WeatherForecast[]>("sample-
data/weather.json");
   string baseURI= UriHelper.GetBaseUri();
}
```

Here, we use the `@inject` keyword in to inject the reference directly to our component. `HttpClient` provides us with the methods with which we can send and receive requests and their responses over the network. `IUriHelper`, on the other hand, provides us with the methods to handle the URI and navigation from one component to another.

Routing in Blazor

Blazor provides the feature to route the user from one page to another by using the built-in routing technique. Let's now learn the different routing techniques of Blazor in detail.

Defining the route for a page

To define the route for a page, we need to use the `@page` directive. As you have already seen in the previous examples, when the value provided in the `@page` directive is appended to the root URL of the application, it will redirect to the corresponding component. We can also use multiple, but distinct `@page` directives for a single component. Take a look at the following code snippet for an example:

```
@page "/route1"
@page "/route2"
<h1> This is a Demo page </h1>
```

This allows us to use multiple routes for a single page. The component defined in the preceding snippet can be accessed by using two routes: `/route1` and `/route2`.

Parameterized routing

We can also pass the parameters to the route. Let's try to understand this with the help of the following code sample:

```
page "/route/{routeparam}"

@*insert HTML DOM here*@

@functions{

    [Parameter]
    private string routeparam { get; set; }
}
```

In the preceding snippet, we defined a `routeparam` string variable and decorated it with the `[Parameter]` attribute. This allows us to use this variable as a route parameter, defined in the `@page` directive.

 The name of the parameter in the `@page` directive must match the name of the variable that has the `[Parameter]` attribute.

To redirect to this page, we need to substitute a string variable in place of `{routeparam}`. Hence, if we append `/route/randomstring` to the base URL, we will be redirected to this page.

Navigation between components

So far, we have discussed routing between the components using the `@page` directive, which defines a fixed route for a page. But how can we navigate from one page to another using C# code? The answer is the `IUriHelper` service, which we already discussed in the previous section.

IUriHelper provides a NavigateTo method, which accepts the route of the page as a parameter and redirects the user from one page to another:

```
@page "/demoapp"
@using Microsoft.AspNetCore.Blazor.Services;
@inject IUriHelper UriHelper

<button class="btn btn-primary" onclick="@NavDemo">Click me</button>

@functions {

void NavDemo()
{
    UriHelper.NavigateTo("counter");
}
```

In this snippet, we injected the IUriHelper service dependency into our component. We also defined a button that will call the NavDemo method when clicked. The NavDemo method will invoke the NavigateTo method by providing the route of the **Counter** page as a parameter. Hence, when the button is clicked, the user will be navigated to the **Counter** page.

NavLink component

Blazor provides us with a NavLink component that can be used in place of the <a> attribute in HTML. It toggles an active CSS class, based on whether or not the current URL matches the href property. This helps the user to understand which pages are active among all of the available navigation links. You can see the use of the NavLink component in the NavMenu.cshtml file of our application, as shown in the following code snippet:

```
<NavLink href="" Match=NavLinkMatch.All>
  <span class="glyphicon glyphicon-home"></span> Home
</NavLink>
```

The Match attribute can have two possible values:

- NavLinkMatch.All: This shows that this particular NavLink should be active, but only if it matches the entire current URL
- NavLinkMatch.Prefix: This shows that this particular NavLink should be active if it matches any prefix of the current URL

Let's examine the use of `NavLinkMatch.Prefix` with the help of an example. Create a new component and declare the route of the page as `fetchdata-all`.

Open the `NavMenu.cshtml` file and add the following NavLink item to it:

```
<li class="nav-item px-3">
  <NavLink class="nav-link" href="fetchdata-all" Match=NavLinkMatch.Prefix>
   <span class="oi oi-list-rich" aria-hidden="true"></span>Fetch data 1
  </NavLink>
</li>
```

We already have a NavLink with the `fetchdata` URL defined. Launch the application and click on the **Fetch data 1** menu item. You can see that both of the navigation links will be highlighted. This shows that both pages have a common prefix in their respective URLs:

Rendering raw HTML

Version 0.5.0 of Blazor introduces a new feature that allows us to render raw HTML on the web page. We can achieve this by using the `MarkupString` property, which is defined in the application's metadata. A variable wrapped with the `MarkupString` property is treated as HTML or SVG, rather than literal text, and is inserted into the application's DOM.

Create a new page in the `Pages` folder, name it `RawHTML.cshtml`, and add the following code into it:

```
@page "/renderhtml"

<h1>Raw HTML Rendering in Blazor</h1>
<hr />

@((MarkupString)customHTML)

@functions {
string customHTML = "<p>This is a <strong>custom HTML</strong> code</p>";
}
```

Add the navigation link to the page in the `NavMenu.cshtml` file and launch the application. You should see a page similar to the one shown in the following screenshot:

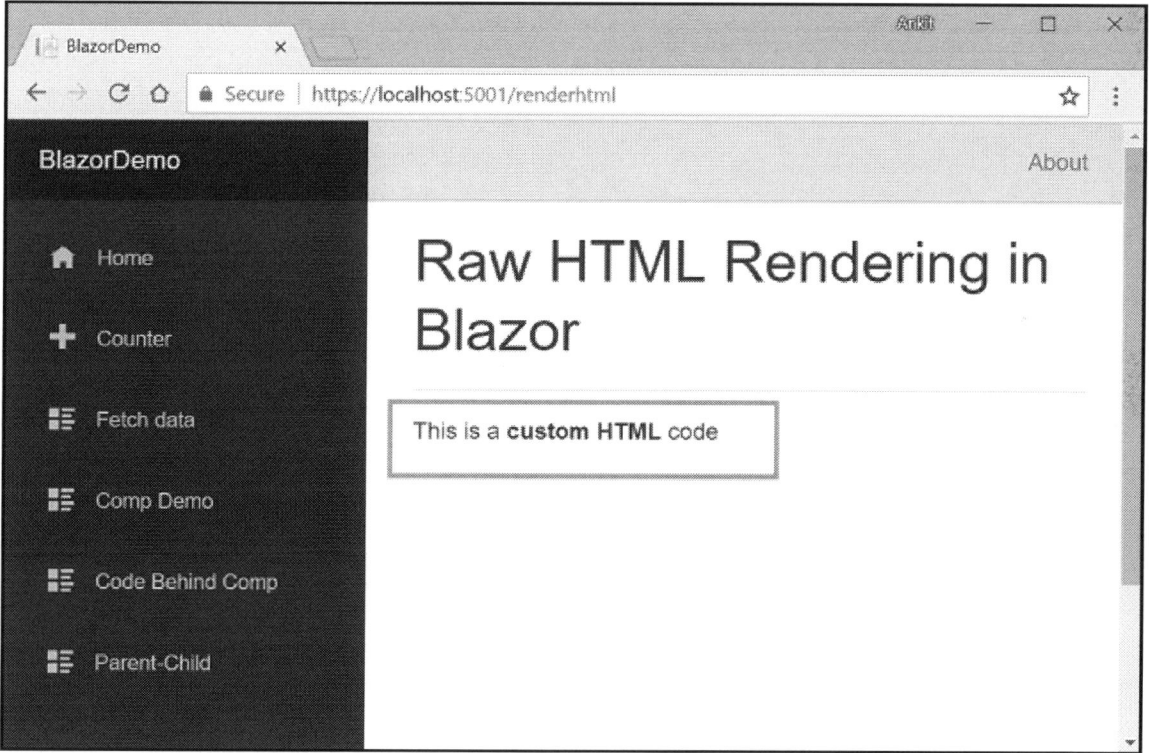

Summary

In this chapter, we learned about the building blocks of Blazor. We learned that Blazor is a component-based framework, and how we can work with Blazor components. We now understand how layouts, data binding, routing, event handling, and dependency injection all work in Blazor. We also learned about rendering raw HTML on the web page, a feature that was introduced as a part of Blazor's 0.5.0 release.

In the next chapter, we will learn about the JavaScript interop feature in Blazor.

3
A Deep Dive into JavaScript Interop

In the previous chapter, we learned that Blazor is a component-based framework and explored some of the basic concepts of the Blazor framework, such as data binding, application life cycle methods, event handling, and so on. In this chapter, we will learn about JavaScript Interop, which is one of the main features provided by the Blazor framework. We will look at what JavaScript Interop is and how to use it in a Blazor application.

In this chapter, we will cover the following topics:

- What is JavaScript Interop?
- How do we call a JavaScript function from C# code?
- Capturing references to HTML elements
- How do we call a C# method from JavaScript code?
- How do we use third-party JS libraries with Blazor?

We will come to understand these concepts with the help of an example application that we will build as we proceed with this chapter.

Technical requirements

You need to have knowledge on following concepts:

- C#
- ASP.NET Core
- Entity Framework Core
- Ado.NET

You should also install following software to start Blazor development.

- .NET Core 2.1 or above SDK.
- Visual Studio Code
- Visual Studio 2017 v15.7 or above
- ASP.NET Core Blazor Language Services extension

The code files of this chapter can be found on GitHub:
```
https://github.com/PacktPublishing/Blazor-Quick-Start-Guide/tree/master/
Chapter03/JsInteropDemo
```

Check out the following video to see the code in action:

```
http://bit.ly/2CQaCwn
```

What is JavaScript Interop?

The Blazor framework mainly uses C# or Razor code to create its components, but there are a few scenarios where we need to access JavaScript, such as the following:

- When accessing browser DOM elements: Blazor uses WebAssembly and Mono runtime for its execution, neither of which have direct access to a browser's DOM; since Blazor is a client-side framework, it needs to access and manipulate the DOM to create a user interface
- When accessing JavaScript APIs: Sometimes, developers want to refer to JavaScript APIs to add a new functionality or to enhance an existing functionality in an application

So, how can Blazor access JavaScript code? The answer to this question is JavaScript Interop. The ability to access a JavaScript method using a high-level language such as C#, and vice versa, is achieved through JavaScript Interop. JavaScript Interop is a feature of WebAssembly, and therefore Blazor is able to implement it.

Creating an example Blazor application

We will learn about the concepts in this chapter with the help of code samples, so we need to create an example Blazor application to write and execute the code as we proceed.

To do this, simply follow the same steps we discussed in the previous chapter and create an example application named `JsInteropDemo`.

Once the `JsInteropDemo` project file has been created, open it using VS code and build the application code using the `dotnet build` command.

Now that's done, let's move on and learn how to call a JS function from C# code within our Blazor component.

How to call a JavaScript function from C# code

To call a JavaScript function from C#, we need to use the `IJSRuntime` abstraction. This is accessible via the `JSRuntime` class and is defined in the framework's metadata. We will then invoke the current method of the `JSRuntime` class using `JSRuntime.Current`, which should generate `Microsoft.JSInterop.IJSRuntime`.

The `IJSRuntime` interface is used to invoke the specified JavaScript function asynchronously. The `InvokeAsync<T>` method defined in `IJSRuntime` will take an identifier for the function to invoke, along with any number of JSON-serializable arguments. The type parameter `T` of the `InvokeAsync<T>` method is the JSON-serializable return type, and this method returns an instance of `T` that's obtained by JSON deserializing the return value.

The `IJSRuntime` abstraction is asynchronous, which allows us to use it for out-of-process scenarios only. However, if an application runs in-process and we want to invoke a JavaScript function synchronously, we need to use the `Invoke<T>` method of the `IJSInProcessRuntime` abstraction.

We can call to our JavaScript function in the following possible ways:

- Without passing any parameters
- By passing parameters

We will discuss both of these methods in detail, but first of all, we need to define our JavaScript methods.

Defining JavaScript methods

We need to ensure the following two things while creating a JavaScript function:

- That our JS code is not written in the `.cshtml` file. Always write JS code in the `wwroot/index.html` file. If you write JS code in the `.cshtml` file, you will get a compile time error.

- That your custom JS code is added in the `<script>` tag after `<script src="_framework/blazor.webassembly.js"></script>` in the `<body>` section of the `wwwroot/index.html` file. This is to ensure that your custom script will execute after the `blazor.webassembly.js` script has been loaded.

Keeping those two points in mind, let's now create two JS functions inside the `index.html` file. Open `wwwroot/index.html` and input the following code in the `<body>` section:

```
<script>
  function showAlertBox() {
    alert("I am invoked from .NET");
  }
  function showPrompt(message) {
    alert("You entered : " + message);
  }
</script>
```

In the preceding code, we have defined the following two methods:

- `showAlertBox()`: This method does not accept any argument and will display a pop-up alert containing a static message
- `showPrompt(message)`: This method will accept an argument and a message, and will display a pop-up alert containing the value passed to the method

Now that we have completed the JS part, we will proceed and code the .NET part.

Calling a JavaScript function without parameters

The syntax to call a JS function without parameters from .NET is as follows:

```
JSRuntime.Current.InvokeAsync<T>("JS function name");
```

Now, let's start creating our component. Create two files in the Pages folder; name them CallJSMethod.cshtml and CallJSMethod.cshtml.cs, respectively.

Open CallJSMethod.cshtml and input the following code:

```
@page "/calljsmethod"
@inherits CallJSMethodModel

<h3>Invoking a JS method WITHOUT PARAMETERS from .NET</h3>
<br />
<button class="btn btn-primary" onclick="@CallJSMethod">Click Me
!!</button>

<hr />
<h3>Invoking a JS method WITH PARAMETERS from .NET</h3>
<br />
```

In the preceding code, we defined one button, which will invoke the CallJSMethod method to call our JS function without parameters.

Now, open CallJSMethod.cshtml.cs and input the following code:

```
using Microsoft.AspNetCore.Blazor.Components;
using Microsoft.JSInterop;
using System;
using System.Collections.Generic;
using System.Linq;
using System.Threading.Tasks;

namespace JsInteropDemo.Pages
{
    public class CallJSMethodModel : BlazorComponent
    {
        protected string message { get; set; }
        protected void CallJSMethod()
        {
            JSRuntime.Current.InvokeAsync<bool>("showAlertBox");
        }
    }
}
```

Here, we have included a reference to the `Microsoft.JSInterop` namespace, which will allow us to use JS Interop functionality. The `CallJSMethod` method will invoke the `showAlertBox` function, but won't take any arguments.

Now, let's look at how to call a JS function with parameters.

Calling a JavaScript function with parameters

The syntax to call a JS function with parameters from .NET is as follows:

```
JSRuntime.Current.InvokeAsync<T>("JS function name", param1, param2);
```

You can pass multiple parameters to JS functions, so we have shown you two to demonstrate this.

Now, add the following lines of code in the `CallJSMethod.cshtml` file:

```
<Input class="col-sm-3" bind="@message" />
<br /><br />
<button class="btn btn-default" onclick="@CallJSMethodWithParams">Show
Prompt</button>
```

Here, we have defined a textbox for reading user input and a corresponding button that will invoke the `CallJSMethodWithParams` method and passed the value entered in the textbox, which will then be displayed as a pop-up alert.

Now, open `CallJSMethod.cshtml.cs` and add the following method definition inside the `CallJSMethodModel` class:

```
protected void CallJSMethodWithParams()
{
    JSRuntime.Current.InvokeAsync<bool>("showPrompt", message);
}
```

`CallJSMethodWithParams` will invoke the `showPrompt` function and will accept one string parameter, which is the value that was entered into the textbox.

Add the navigation link to this page in the `NavMenu.cshtml` file and run the application by using the `dotnet run` command. Navigate to the `/calljsmethod` page and you should see a web page like the one shown in the following screenshot:

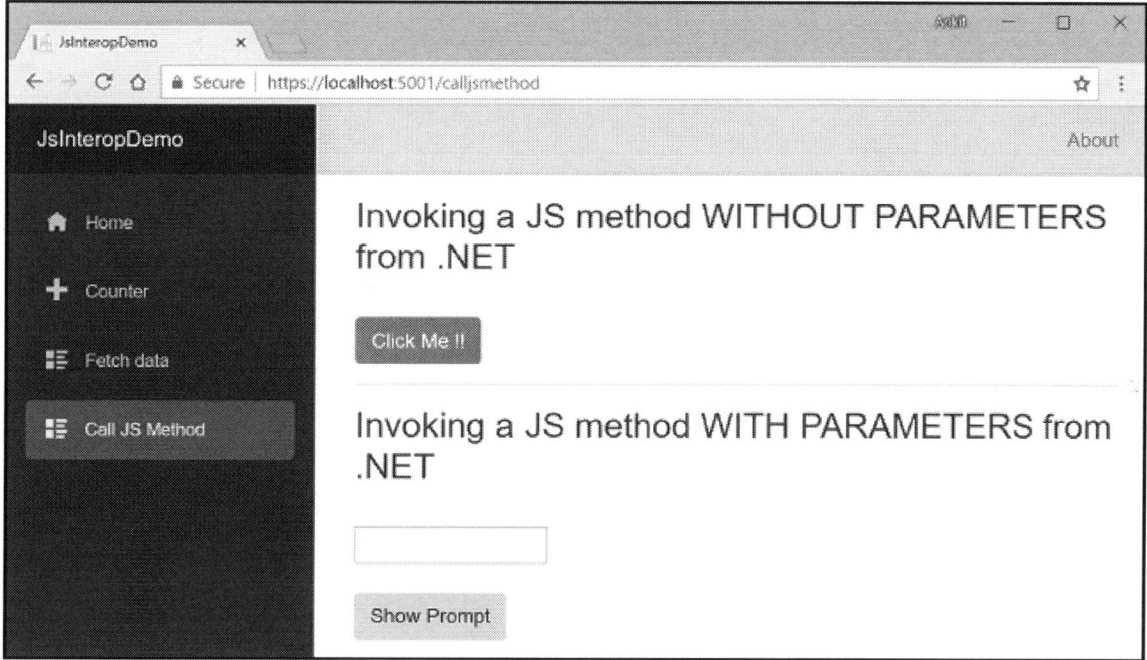

Click on the **Click me !!** button. This will open a pop-up showing a static message, as defined in the JS function, as you can see in the following screenshot:

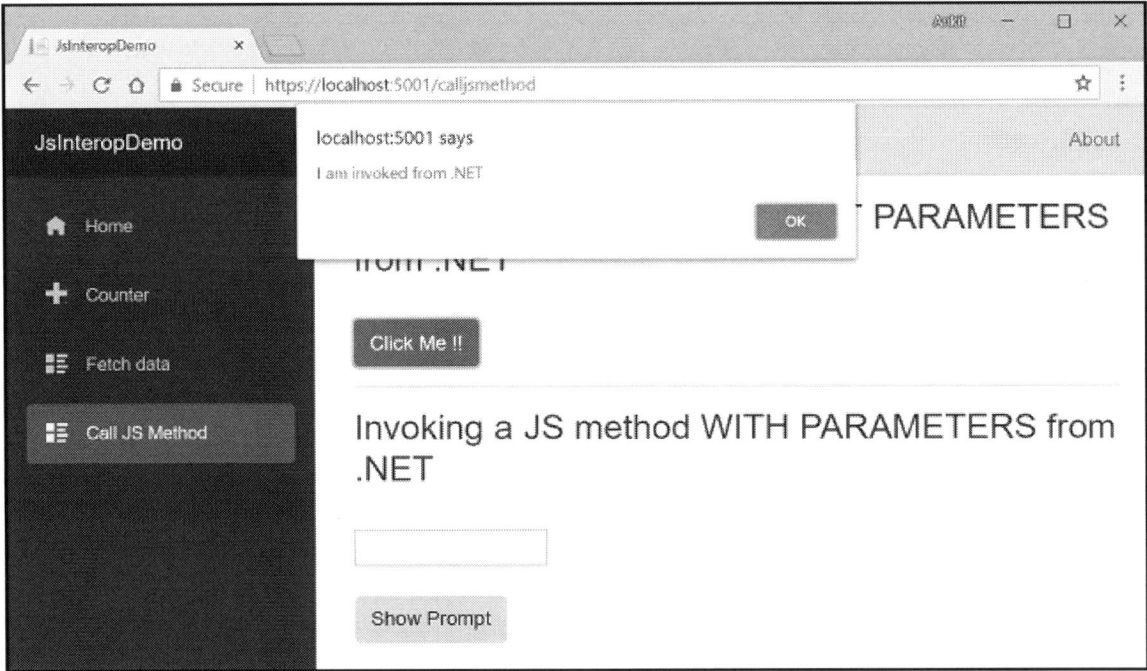

Again, enter some text in the input box and click on the **Show Prompt** button. It will display a pop-up showing the text you entered in the input box, as shown in the following screenshot:

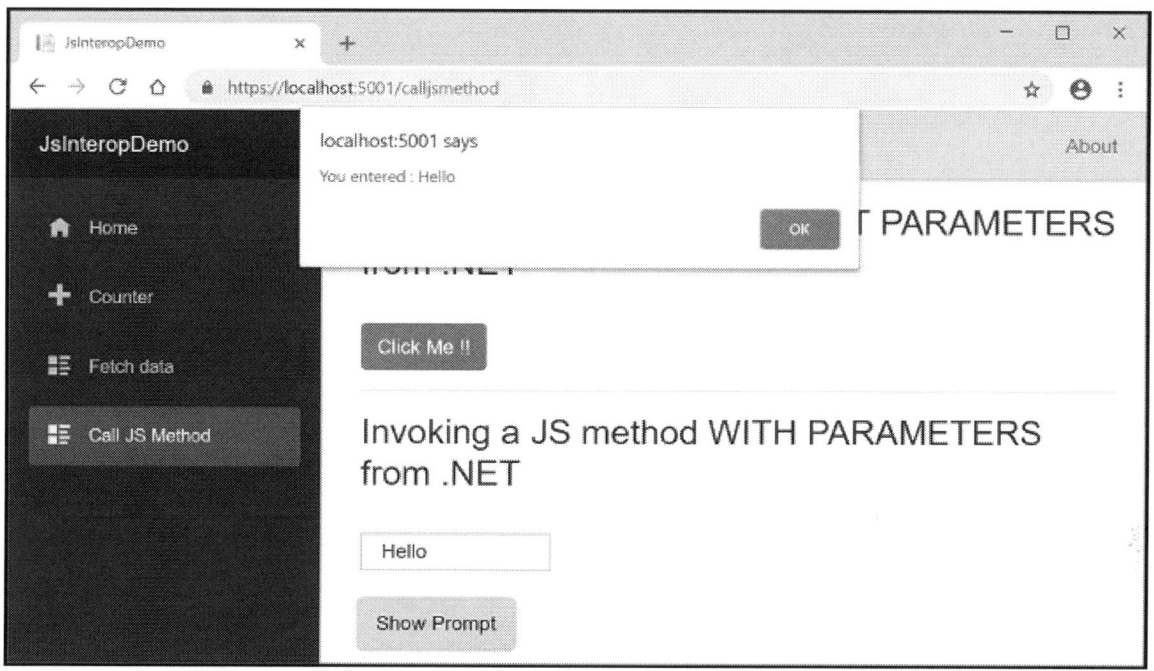

Capturing references to HTML elements

Sometimes, we need to capture references to HTML elements inside our JS code. For example, a JS API might need to call commands such as focus, blur, or innerText on an HTML element. Blazor allows us to capture references to HTML elements in a component. To achieve this, we need to add a ref attribute to the HTML element and then define a field of type ElementRef, whose name matches with the value of the ref attribute.

ElementRef represents a reference to a rendered element, and it can only be passed to our JS code with the use JavaScript Interop. The JS code will receive an HTMLElement instance, which can then be used with normal DOM APIs.

Let's take a look at an example; open the index.html file and add the following JS function into it:

```
<script>
  function showValue(element) {
    alert(element.value);
  }
</script>
```

The preceding function will access the value of the HTML element using the value property and display it in a pop-up.

The next step is to create the component by adding two files, `ElementRefDemo.cshtml` and `ElementRefDemo.cshtml.cs`, into our `Pages` folder.

So, open `ElementRefDemo.cshtml.cs` and input the following code:

```
using Microsoft.AspNetCore.Blazor;
using Microsoft.AspNetCore.Blazor.Components;
using Microsoft.JSInterop;
using System;
using System.Linq;
using System.Threading.Tasks;

namespace JsInteropDemo.Pages
{
    public static class ElementRefDemoExtension
    {
        public static Task GetValue(this ElementRef elementRef)
        {
            return JSRuntime.Current.InvokeAsync<object>("showValue",
elementRef);
        }
    }

    public class ElementRefDemoModel : BlazorComponent
    {
        public ElementRef inputRef;
        public void getInputValue()
        {
            inputRef.GetValue();
        }
    }
}
```

Here, we defined an `ElementRefDemoExtension` class to define our extension method, `GetValue`. This method will invoke our JS function `showValue` and pass the reference of the HTML element as a parameter. In the `ElementRefDemoModel` class, we declared a variable called `inputRef` of the type `ElementRef`. We then call our `GetValue` method on the variable inside the `getInputValue` method, which is invoked with a button click.

Now, open `ElementRefDemo.cshtml` and input the following code:

```
@page "/elementrefdemo"
@inherits ElementRefDemoModel

<h2>Capturing references to HTML elements</h2>
<hr/>

<input class="col-sm-3" type="text" ref="inputRef"/>
<button class="btn btn-default" onclick="@getInputValue">Get Value</button>
```

Here, we have defined an input element and added a `ref` attribute to it. The `ref` attribute has the same name as the variable of type `ElementRef`, as defined in the `ElementRefDemo.cshtml.cs` file. The **Get Value** button will call the `getInputValue` method with a click, which will then invoke our JS function `showValue` to display the value entered into the textbox via a pop-up.

Add the navigation link to this page in the `NavMenu.cshtml` file and run the application by using the `dotnet run` command. Navigate to the `/elementrefdemo` page, which should generate the following screenshot:

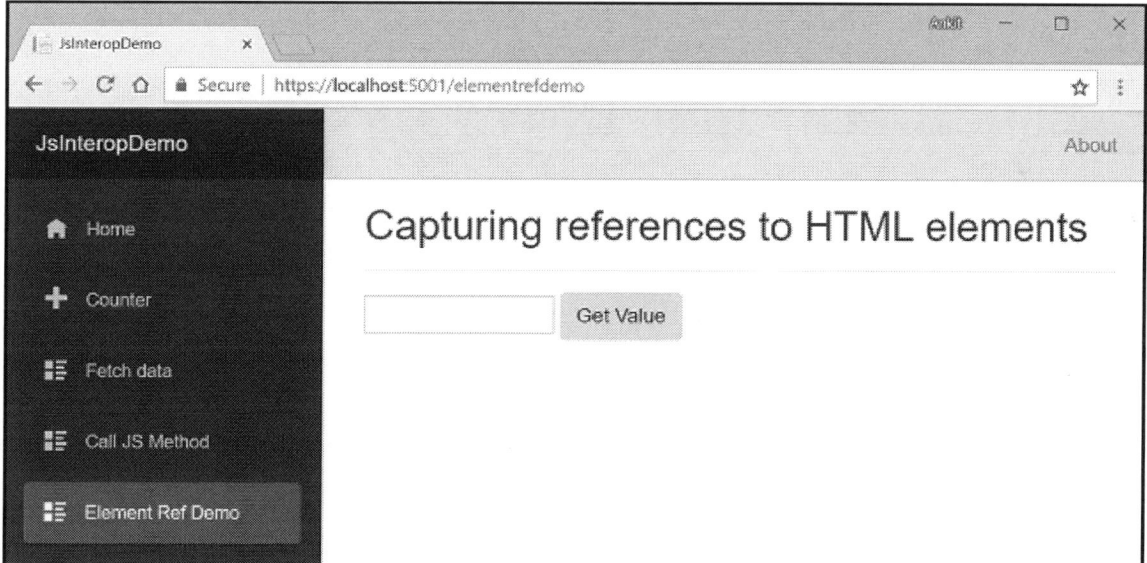

Type something in the textbox and click on the `Get Value` button. You should see a pop-up that displays the value entered in the textbox, as shown in the following screenshot:

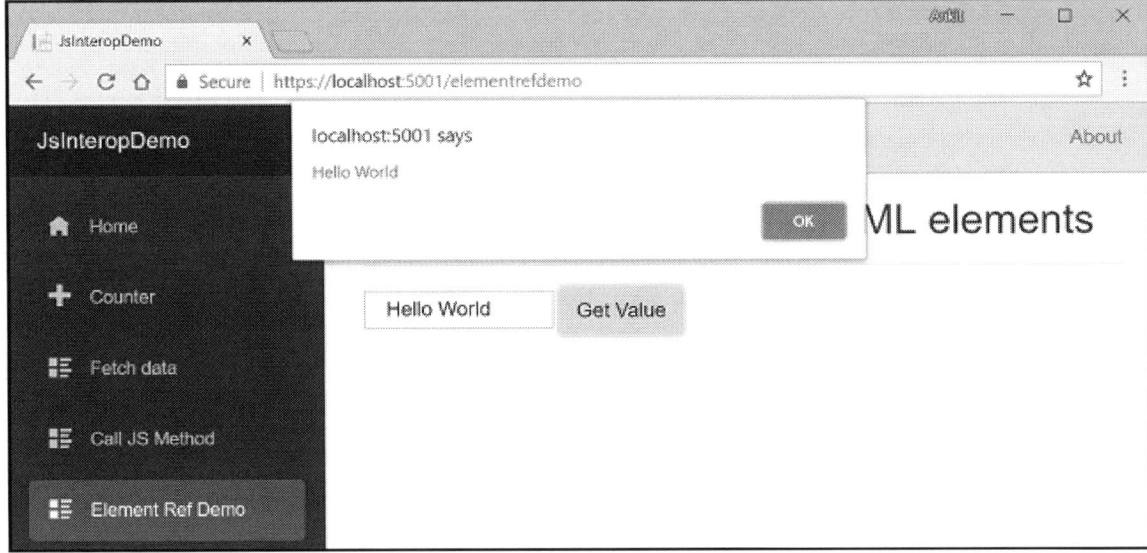

Calling a C# method from JavaScript code

Blazor allows us to invoke a C# method from JS code. To invoke a .NET method from JavaScript, use the `DotNet.invokeMethod` function to call a method synchronously, or the `DotNet.invokeMethodAsync` function to make an asynchronous call.

The syntax for calling a C# method from JavaScript is as follows:

```
DotNet.invokeMethodAsync('C# method assembly name', 'C# Method Name');
```

To invoke a C# or .NET method from JavaScript, the target .NET method must meet the following criteria:

- It must be declared as public static
- It should have no overloads
- The method must be non-generic (calling a generic method is not supported as of Blazor 0.6.0, but is expected to be included in future releases)
- It must have concrete JSON serializable parameter types
- It should be decorated with the `[JSInvokable]` attribute

Now, open `wwwroot/index.html` and add the following JS function definition to it:

```
<script>
  function callCSFunction() {
    DotNet.invokeMethodAsync('JsInteropDemo', 'CSCallBackMethodAsync');
  }
</script>
```

As you can see, the `callCSFunction` function will invoke our C# method, `CSCallBackMethodAsync`, using the `invokeMethodAsync` function. In the preceding code, we also passed the assembly name of our C# method, which is `JsInteropDemo`.

Now let's create our component to get a better understanding of what happens. Create two files, `CallCSMethod.cshtml` and `CallCSMethod.cshtml.cs`, in the `Pages` folder.

Now, open the `CallCSMethod.cshtml` file and input the following code:

```
@page "/csdemo"
@inherits CallCSMethodModel

<h1>Invoking CS method from JavaScript</h1>

<button class="btn btn-primary" onclick="@invokeJSMethod">Call C#
Method</button>
<br />
<br />
<p>@message</p>
```

Here, we defined a button that will call the `invokeJSMethod` function to invoke a JS function. This JS function will then invoke a C# method, which will set the value of a string parameter message, which, in turn, will be displayed on a web page to show that our function call was successful.

Now, open the `CallCSMethod.cshtml.cs` file and input the following code:

```
using Microsoft.AspNetCore.Blazor.Components;
using Microsoft.JSInterop;
using System;
using System.Collections.Generic;
using System.Linq;
using System.Threading.Tasks;

namespace JsInteropDemo.Pages
{
    public class CallCSMethodModel : BlazorComponent
```

```
    {
        protected static string message { get; set; }
        protected void invokeJSMethod()
        {
            JSRuntime.Current.InvokeAsync<bool>("callCSFunction");
        }

        [JSInvokable]
        public static void CSCallBackMethodAsync()
        {
            message = "C# Method invoked";
        }
    }
}
```

As you can see in the preceding snippet, the invokeJSMethod method calls the callCSFunction function in JS, which, in turn, invokes the CSCallBackMethodAsync method to set the value of our string variable message. CSCallBackMethodAsync is decorated with the [JSInvokable] attribute so that it can be invoked by a JS function.

We need to ensure the following things before invoking the method:

- If we do not use the [JSInvokable] attribute on the method that is being invoked from JS, we will get a runtime error
- If two methods with the same name are present in one assembly and only one of them has the [JSInvokable] attribute, that method will be invoked from JS and there will be no error
- If two methods with the same name are present in one assembly and both of them have a [JSInvokable] attribute, this results in a runtime error

Now, add the navigation link to this page in the NavMenu.cshtml file and run the application by using the dotnet run command. Navigate to /csdemo page, where you should see a page similar to the one shown in the following screenshot:

Now click on the **Call C# Method** button. It will display a message beneath the button, as shown in the following screenshot:

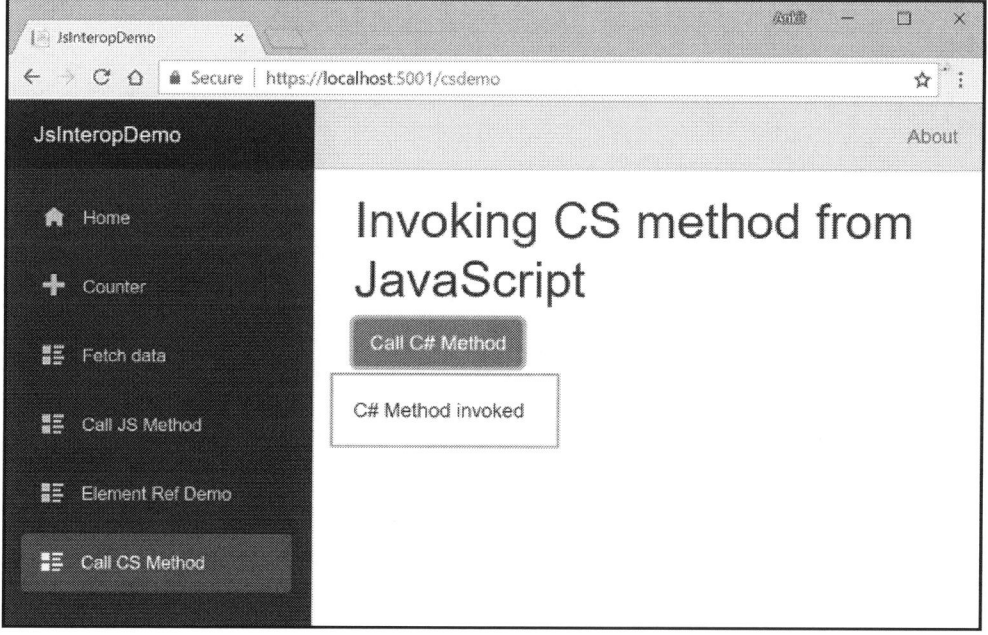

Blazor 0.5.0 introduces the functionality of calling .NET instance methods from JavaScript. To invoke a .NET instance method from JS, we need to first pass it to JS by wrapping it in a `DotNetObjectRef` instance. The .NET instance is then passed by reference to JS and allows us to invoke .NET instance methods on the instance by using the `invokeMethod` or `invokeMethodAsync` functions.

Now, add two files, `InvokeInstanceMethod.cshtml` and `InvokeInstanceMethod.cshtml.cs`, to create a component.

Open `InvokeInstanceMethod.cshtml` and input the following code:

```
@page "/instancedemo"
@inherits InvokeInstanceMethodModel

<h1>Invoke .NET instance method</h1>

<hr />

<button class="btn btn-primary" onclick="@DisplayMessage">Show
Message</button>
```

Here, we defined a button that will call the `DisplayMessage` method.

Now, open `InvokeInstanceMethod.cshtml.cs` and input the following code:

```
using Microsoft.AspNetCore.Blazor.Components;
using Microsoft.JSInterop;
using System;
using System.Collections.Generic;
using System.Linq;
using System.Threading.Tasks;

namespace JsInteropDemo.Pages
{
    public class HelloWorld
    {
        [JSInvokable]
        public string showMessege() => $"Hello World";
    }
    public class InvokeInstanceMethodModel : BlazorComponent
    {
        public static Task DisplayMessage()
        {
            return JSRuntime.Current.InvokeAsync<object>(
                "callInstanceMethod",
                new DotNetObjectRef(new HelloWorld()));
        }
```

```
          }
     }
```

In the preceding code, we defined a class, HelloWorld, with a JSInvokable method and showMessege to return a sample message. In the DisplayMessage method, we called a JS function, callInstanceMethod, and passed an instance of the HelloWorld class to it by wrapping it in a DotNetObjectRef instance.

Now, open index.html and add the following piece of code to it:

```
<script>
    function callInstanceMethod(dotnetHelper) {
        return dotnetHelper.invokeMethodAsync('showMessege')
            .then(r => alert(r));
    }
</script>
```

This preceding method will receive an instance of the HelloWorld object and will then invoke the showMessege method of the HelloWorld class. The string value returned by the showMessege method will be displayed with a pop-up alert.

Run the application and click on the **Show Message** button to display the pop-up message, as shown in the following screenshot:

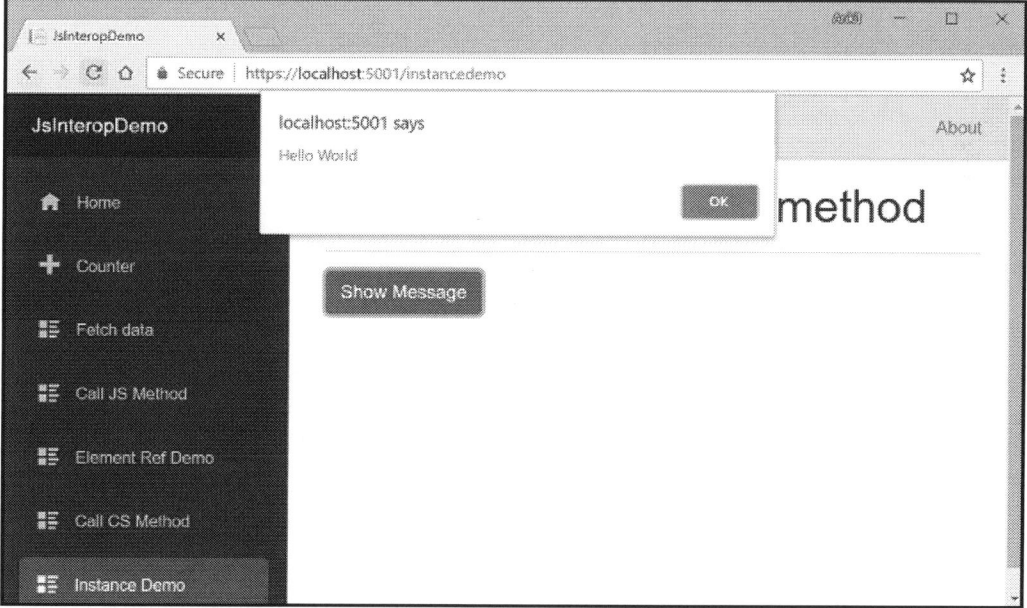

Using third-party JS libraries

Until now, we have learned how to invoke a JS method from a C# method and vice versa using JavaScript Interop. Sometimes, however, we may need to use a third-party JS library in our application to enhance user experience. We can show graphs, grids, and even animation using open source JS libraries.

In this section, we will learn how to use jsGrid, a lightweight grid jQuery plugin. jsGrid displays data in a grid and offers many built-in features, such as sorting, filtering, pagination, and inline editing, that can be used on data. You can visit http://js-grid.com/ to learn more about the jsGrid library.

It's now time to create components by adding the JsGridDemo.cshtml and JsGridDemo.cshtml.cs files in the Pages folder.

Open the JsGridDemo.cshtml file and input the following code:

```
@page "/jsgriddemo"
@inherits JsGridDemoModel

<h1>Display data using JS Grid</h1>
<hr />

<button class="btn btn-primary" onclick="@ShowGrid">Show Grid</button>
<br/>
<br/>
<div id="dataGrid"></div>
```

Here, we defined a button that will invoke the ShowGrid method to display data using jsGrid. We also defined a <div> element that will be used as jsGrid.

Next, input the following code in to the JsGridDemo.cshtml.cs file:

```
using Microsoft.AspNetCore.Blazor.Components;
using Microsoft.JSInterop;
using System;
using System.Collections.Generic;
using System.Linq;
using System.Threading.Tasks;

namespace JsInteropDemo.Pages
{
    public class JsGridDemoModel : BlazorComponent
    {
        public static void ShowGrid()
        {
```

```
                    JSRuntime.Current.InvokeAsync<bool>("showJsGrid");
            }
        }
}
```

In the preceding code, we defined the ShowGrid method, which will invoke our JS function showJsGrid to display the jsGrid on the UI.

Now, we will define our JS code in the wwwroot/index.html file.

The first step for this is to add the CDN reference to the JQuery and jsGrid libraries. So, add the following lines of code in the <head> section of the index.html page:

```
<script
src="https://ajax.googleapis.com/ajax/libs/jquery/3.3.1/jquery.min.js"></sc
ript>
<link type="text/css" rel="stylesheet"
href="https://cdnjs.cloudflare.com/ajax/libs/jsgrid/1.5.3/jsgrid.min.css"
/>
<link type="text/css" rel="stylesheet"
href="https://cdnjs.cloudflare.com/ajax/libs/jsgrid/1.5.3/jsgrid-theme.min.
css" />
<script type="text/javascript"
src="https://cdnjs.cloudflare.com/ajax/libs/jsgrid/1.5.3/jsgrid.min.js"></s
cript>
```

Add the following lines of code in the <body> section of the index.html page:

```
<script>
    function showJsGrid() {

        var clients = [
            { "Name": "Harry", "Age": 28, "Country": "Canada", "Married":
false },
            { "Name": "Johny", "Age": 35, "Country": "France", "Married":
true },
            { "Name": "Leena", "Age": 39, "Country": "USA", "Married":
false },
            { "Name": "Rohit", "Age": 26, "Country": "India", "Married":
true },
            { "Name": "Diana", "Age": 32, "Country": "Scotland", "Married":
false }
        ];

        $("#dataGrid").jsGrid({
            width: "500px",
            height: "210px",
            sorting: true,
```

```
                    paging: true,
                    pageSize: 3,
                    pageButtonCount: 3,

                    data: clients,

                    fields: [
                        { name: "Name", type: "text", width: 100},
                        { name: "Age", type: "number", width: 50 },
                        { name: "Country", type: "text", width: 100 },
                        { name: "Married", type: "checkbox", title: "Is Married",
        sorting: false }
                    ]
                });
        }
    </script>
```

Here, we defined the showJsGrid function that will initialize a static set of JSON data and then used the <div> element with the ID dataGrid to display the data using jsGrid's library. We also set the value of the sorting and paging facility as true to allow for the sorting and pagination of the data grid.

In this demo app, we used static JSON data, but you can also use dynamic data from a database. You need to pass a database model object to a JS function and then bind it to jsGrid to do so.

Now, run the application and click on the **Show Grid** button to display the data using jsGrid. You can observe the pagination provided by the grid, and if you click on the column header, it will sort the column values, as shown in the following screenshot:

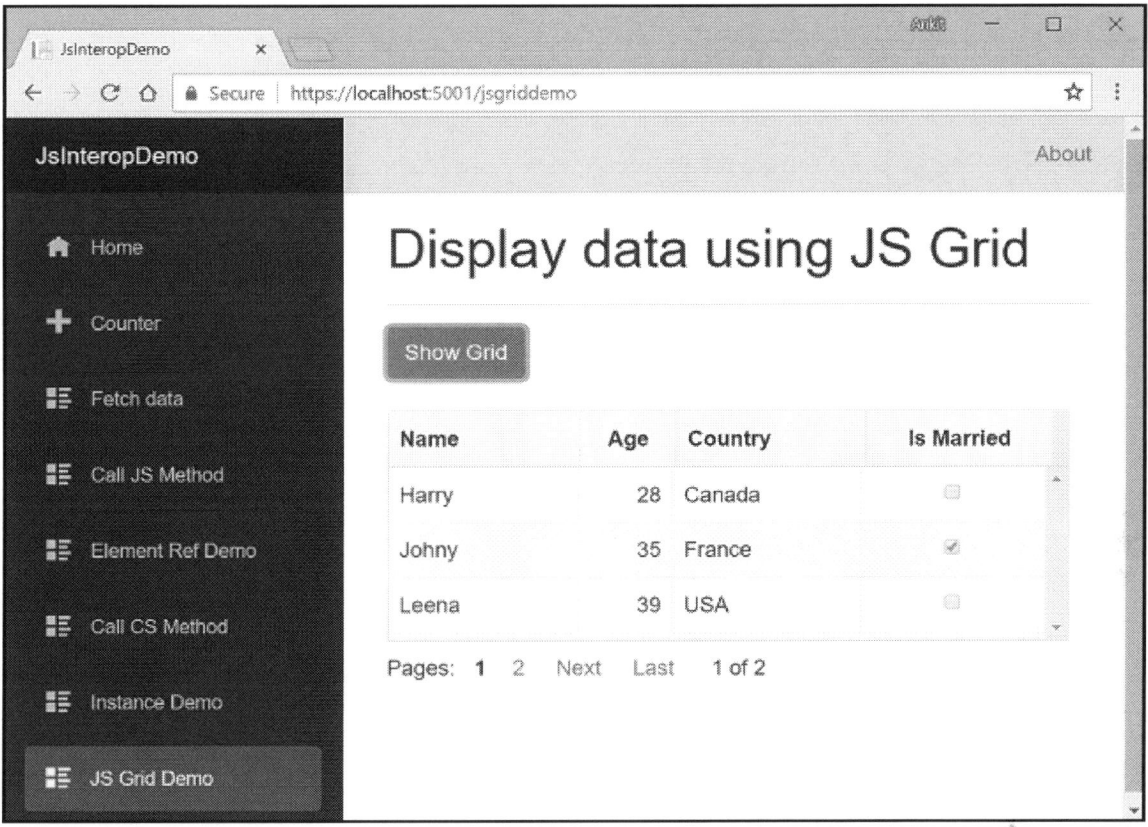

The JS Interop feature allows us to integrate third-party JS libraries into our application. Similar to `jsGrid` library, we can also use other libraries with Blazor, such as Highcharts, Chart.js, and KendoUI.

Summary

In this chapter, we learned about JavaScript Interop, which is one of the most important features provided by the Blazor framework. JavaScript Interop allows us to call a JS function from C# code and vice versa. We also created an example application using jsGrid library to demonstrate how we can use any third-party library in our Blazor application.

In the next chapter, we will create a client-side application using Blazor with the help of Visual Studio 2017.

4
Getting Started with Blazor Using Visual Studio 2017

In the previous chapters, we learned about the core concepts of the Blazor framework and created a few sample applications using Visual Studio Code to help us understand those concepts. We used command-line tools to build and run our applications.

In this chapter, we will learn how to work with Blazor using **Visual Studio (VS)** 2017. VS 2017 provides us with user-friendly methods to create, build, and execute Blazor applications with easy-to-use UI interactions. We will set up the VS 2017 development environment on our machine, and create two client-side applications using Blazor. These applications will be **Single Page Applications (SPAs)** and will run entirely on the browser without any server or database interactions.

We will explore the following topics in detail:

- Setting up the Blazor development environment using Visual Studio 2017
- Creating a Tic-Tac-Toe game
- Creating a basic calculator app

Technical requirements

You need to have knowledge on following concepts:

- C#
- ASP.NET Core
- Entity Framework Core
- Ado.NET

You should also install following software to start Blazor development.

- .NET Core 2.1 or above SDK.
- Visual Studio Code
- Visual Studio 2017 v15.7 or above
- ASP.NET Core Blazor Language Services extension

The code files of this chapter can be found on GitHub:
`https://github.com/PacktPublishing/Blazor-Quick-Start-Guide/tree/master/`
`Chapter04`

Check out the following video to see the code in action:

`http://bit.ly/2Q26oWs`

Setting up the Blazor development environment using Visual Studio 2017

I am using a 64-bit Windows 10 machine, but you can follow the same setup process for other operating systems, including macOS and Linux.

We need to fulfill the following three criteria before we can create a Blazor application using VS 2017:

- Download and install the .NET Core SDK (version 2.1 or above) from `https://www.microsoft.com/net/download/`.
- Download and install VS 2017 (version 15.7 or above) from `https://visualstudio.microsoft.com/downloads/`.
- Download and install the ASP.NET Core Blazor Language Services extension from `https://marketplace.visualstudio.com/items?itemName=aspnet.blazor`.

The Blazor Language Services extension will be downloaded as a file with the `.vsix` extension. Installing this will provide Blazor application templates in VS.

 Versions of VS 2017 below 15.7 do not support the Blazor framework. Therefore, make sure that your VS 2017 version is 15.7 or above.

After we have installed all the three requirements mentioned above, we will proceed to create our first Blazor application using VS 2017.

Creating a Tic-Tac-Toe game using Blazor

Open VS and navigate to **File | New | Project**. It will open a **New Project** dialog. Select **.NET Core** inside the Visual C# menu from the left panel, and then **ASP.NET Core Web Application** from available project types. Put the project name in the **Name** field as **TicTacToe**. Refer to the following screenshot:

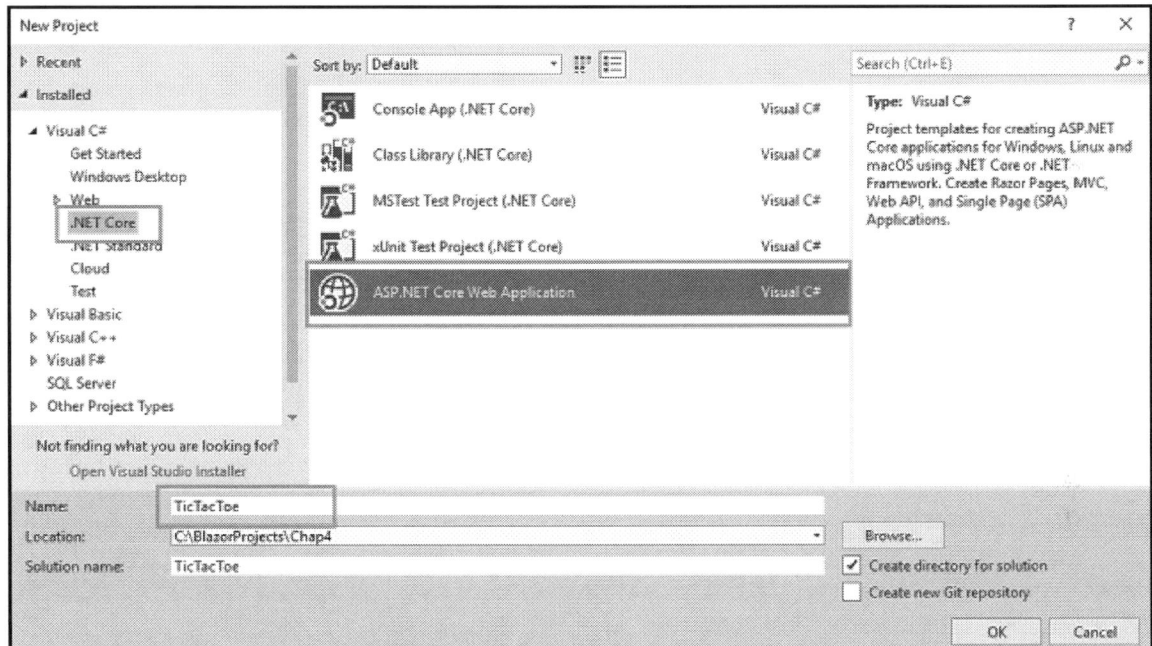

After you click on **OK**, a new dialog will open, asking you to select the project template. There are drop-down menus at the top-left of the template window. From these drop-down menus, select **.NET Core** and **ASP.NET Core 2.1**. You can see three Blazor project templates in this dialog. To create a client-side Blazor application, select the template named `Blazor` and press **OK**. Refer to the following screenshot:

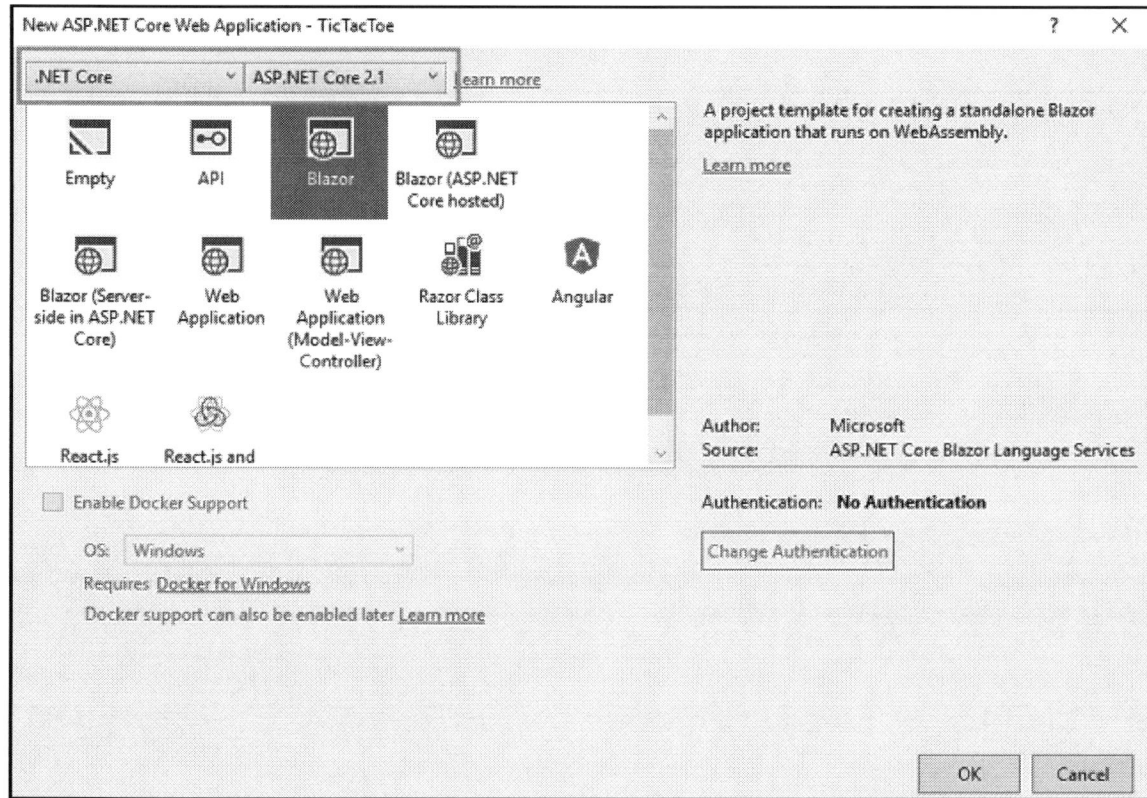

This will create our Blazor application. You can observe the folder structure of the application, as shown in the following screenshot:

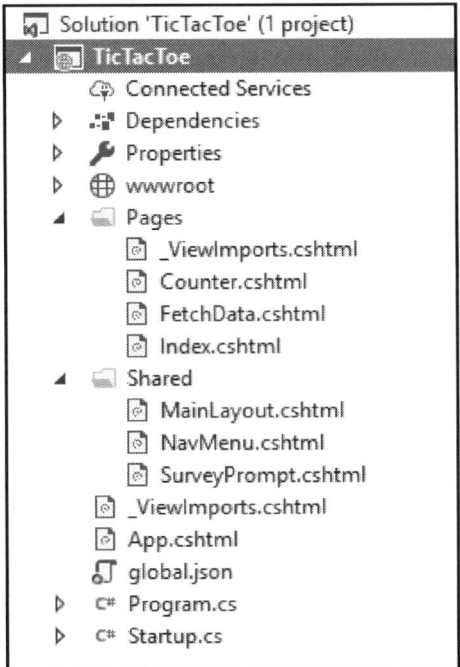

This application has the same folder structure as the applications that we created in previous chapters.

Let's understand the game logic that we will be applying here. We will create a game board in the form of a matrix, consisting of nine buttons. We will bind this matrix to a two-dimensional array, which will hold the value of each cell and can have two values of either **X** or **O**. Player **X** will always take the first turn, and the players will take turns after every move. When the player clicks on the cell to make a move, it will trigger a button click event that will update the value in the two-dimensional array, and simultaneously bind it to the UI. We will then check for the win condition. If the current move results in a win, then we will stop the game; otherwise, the game continues.

Creating the components

For the Tic-Tac-Toe game application, we will use the **code behind file** component structure. This is just to keep the view and logic separated for easy maintenance of our application.

To create our component, right-click on the `TicTacToe/Pages` folder, and then select **Add | New Item**. An **Add New Item** dialog box will open, asking you to select the desired item template from the provided list of items. Select **ASP.NET Core** from the left panel, and then select **Razor Page** from the templates panel. Put the name of file as `tictactoe.cshtml` and click **Add**. Refer to the following screenshot:

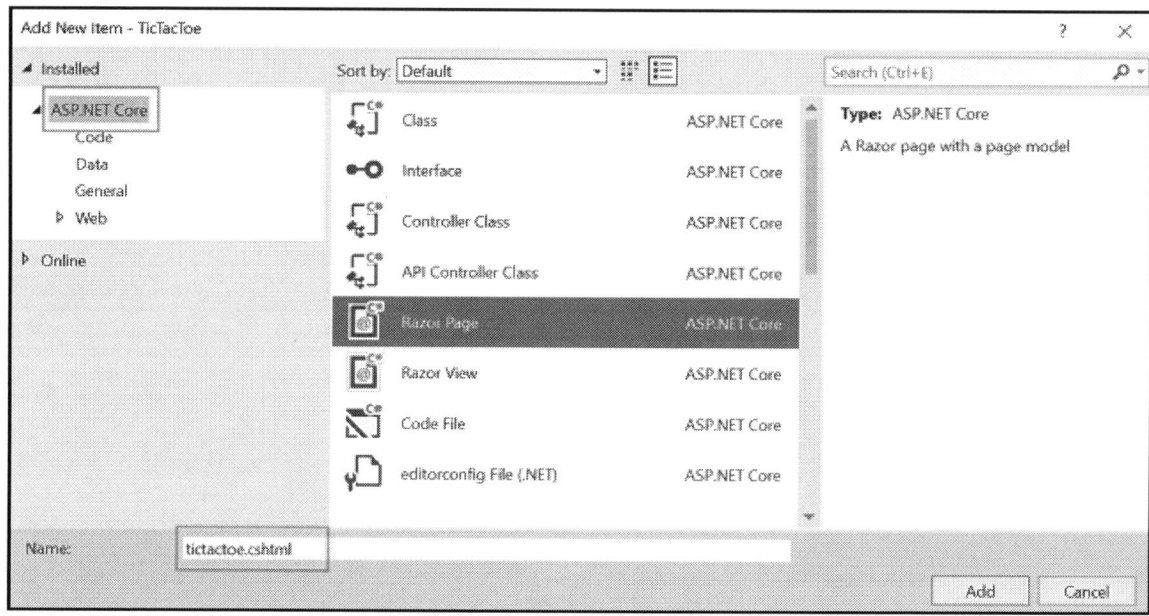

This will create our Razor page with two files: `tictactoe.cshtml` and `tictactoe.cshtml.cs`.

Implementing the game logic

We will now write the code to implement our game logic. Open `tictactoe.cshtml.cs` and enter the following code into the file:

```
using Microsoft.AspNetCore.Blazor.Components;
using System;
using System.Collections.Generic;
using System.Linq;
using System.Threading.Tasks;

namespace TicTacToe.Pages
{
```

```
public class tictactoeModel : BlazorComponent
{
    protected char currentPlayer { get; set; }
    protected char winner { get; set; }
    protected bool win { get; set; } = false;
    protected int[] gameBoard = new int[3] { 0, 1, 2 };
    protected char[,] cellValue = new char[3, 3];

    protected override async Task OnInitAsync()
    {
        await Task.Run(() =>
        {
            ResetGame();
        });
    }

    protected void ResetGame()
    {
        currentPlayer = 'X';
        this.win = false;

        Array.Clear(cellValue, 0, cellValue.Length);
    }
}
}
```

Here, we defined a `tictactoeModel` class, which inherits from the `BlazorComponent` class, an optional base class for Blazor components. This allows the `tictactoeModel` class to act as a Blazor component.

Inside the `tictactoeModel` class, we defined the following five variables:

- `currentPlayer`: A character property used to denote the player that will make the next move in the game. It can have one of two values: **X** or **O**.
- `winner`: A character property to show the winner of the game. It can also have one of two values: **X** or **O**.
- `win`: This is a Boolean property that tracks whether a winning situation has been reached in the game. It is initialized as false.
- `gameBoard`: This is an integer array, used to generate the game board matrix on the UI.
- `cellValue`: This is our two-dimensional character array, used to bind the values to the game board matrix.

Inside the `OnInitAsync` method, we call the `ResetGame` method. The `ResetGame` method will set the current move to player **X** and reset the board.

Furthermore, add the following method definition to the `tictactoeModel` class:

```
protected bool GameWon()
{
  for (int i = 0; i < 3; i++)
  {
    // Check for winning on row
    if ((cellValue[i, 0] == cellValue[i, 1]) && (cellValue[i, 1] ==
cellValue[i, 2]) && cellValue[i, 0] != '\0')
    {
      win = true;
    }
    // Check for winning on column
    else if ((cellValue[0, i] == cellValue[1, i]) && (cellValue[1, i] ==
cellValue[2, i]) && cellValue[0, i] != '\0')
    {
      win = true;
    }
  }

  // Check for winning on diagonal
  if ((cellValue[0, 0] == cellValue[1, 1]) && (cellValue[1, 1] ==
cellValue[2, 2]) && cellValue[0, 0] != '\0')
  {
    win = true;

  }
  else if ((cellValue[0, 2] == cellValue[1, 1]) && (cellValue[1, 1] ==
cellValue[2, 0]) && cellValue[0, 2] != '\0')
  {
    win = true;
  }

  return win;
}
```

Here, we defined a GameWon method, which will check for a win condition on the game board. A win condition in a Tic-Tac-Toe game is achieved when three adjacent cells have the same values either vertically, horizontally, or diagonally. Our method will check for all three of these conditions, and set the value of the win property to true if any of the three criteria match.

Finally, add the following method definition to the `tictactoeModel` class:

```
protected void SetCellValue(int row, int col)
{
  if (cellValue[row, col] == '\0' && !GameWon())
```

```
  {
    cellValue[row, col] = currentPlayer;
    if (GameWon())
    {
      winner = currentPlayer;
    }
    currentPlayer = (currentPlayer == 'X') ? 'O' : 'X';
  }
}
```

The `SetCellValue` method will be invoked when the user clicks on any cell on the game board. It will accept two arguments, which denote the position of the button clicked. It will then set the value at the same position on the two-dimensional array as the current player value, if the current cell is empty and a win situation has not arrived. This denotes that a move has been made in the game, and updates the value in the cell with **X** or **O** values, depending on the player who made the move. We will then check for the win condition, and if the win has been achieved, then we will set the winner value. Before exiting the method, we also switch player's turns using a ternary operator.

Creating the application's UI

To create the UI of the application, open the `tictactoe.cshtml` file and enter the following code:

```
@page "/tic-tac-toe"
@inherits tictactoeModel

<h1>Tic-Tac-Toe Using Blazor</h1>
<hr />

<div class="container" style="background-color:slategray; border:1px solid
black; width:225px">

    @foreach (int row in gameBoard)
    {
        <div>
            @foreach (int col in gameBoard)
            {
                <button class="btn btn-default"
style="width:50px;height:50px;margin: 5px;"
                        onclick=@(() => SetCellValue(row,col))>
                    @cellValue[row, col]
                </button>
            }
        </div>
```

```
    }
</div>
<br />
<div style="text-align:center;">
    <button class="btn btn-info col-sm-3 col-md-3"
onclick="@ResetGame">Reset</button>
</div>
<hr />

@if (!win)
{
    <strong>Player '@currentPlayer' turn.</strong>
}
else
{
    <strong>Player '@winner' has won the game.</strong>
}
```

Here, at the top, we set the route of the page, and also inherit the `tictactoeModel` component class. We use a nested `foreach` loop to create the game board as a matrix of buttons. We will bind the `SetCellValue` method with the button click event. The value of the button text is set to the value of our `cellValue` two-dimensional array. When a user clicks on any cell, the value of the `cellValue` array will be updated, and will bind to the game board to show that a move has been made.

At the end of the preceding code block, we check whether the win situation has been achieved or not, then, in the event of no win, we show the name of the player whose move is next; if a win has been achieved, then we display the name of the winner.

Adding a navigation link

Before executing the application, add the following navigation link to the `NavMenu.cshtml` file:

```
<li class="nav-item px-3">
  <NavLink class="nav-link" href="tic-tac-toe">
    <span class="oi oi-plus" aria-hidden="true"></span> Tic Tac Toe
  </NavLink>
</li>
```

Running the application

Press *F5* to run the application. It will launch the application in your default browser. Click on the **Tic Tac Toe** link in the navigation menu on the left. You should see a page similar to the following screenshot:

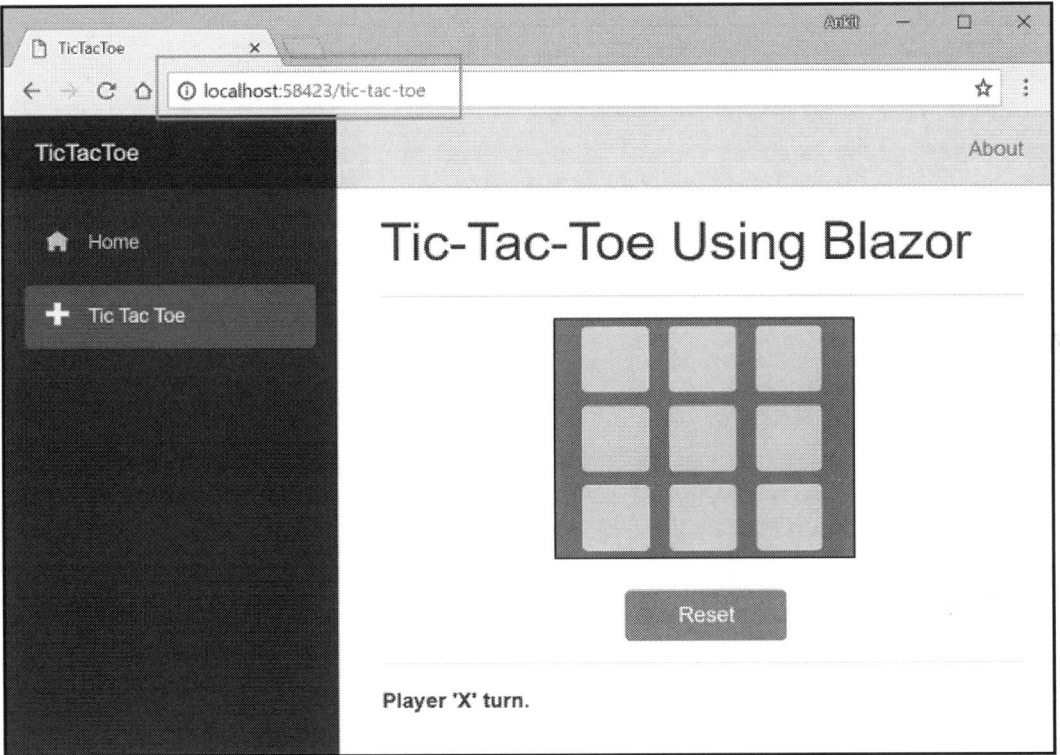

It will display an empty Tic-Tac-Toe game board. Player **X** will make the first move. Click on any cell and the cell value will update to **X**, denoting a move. Refer to the following screenshot:

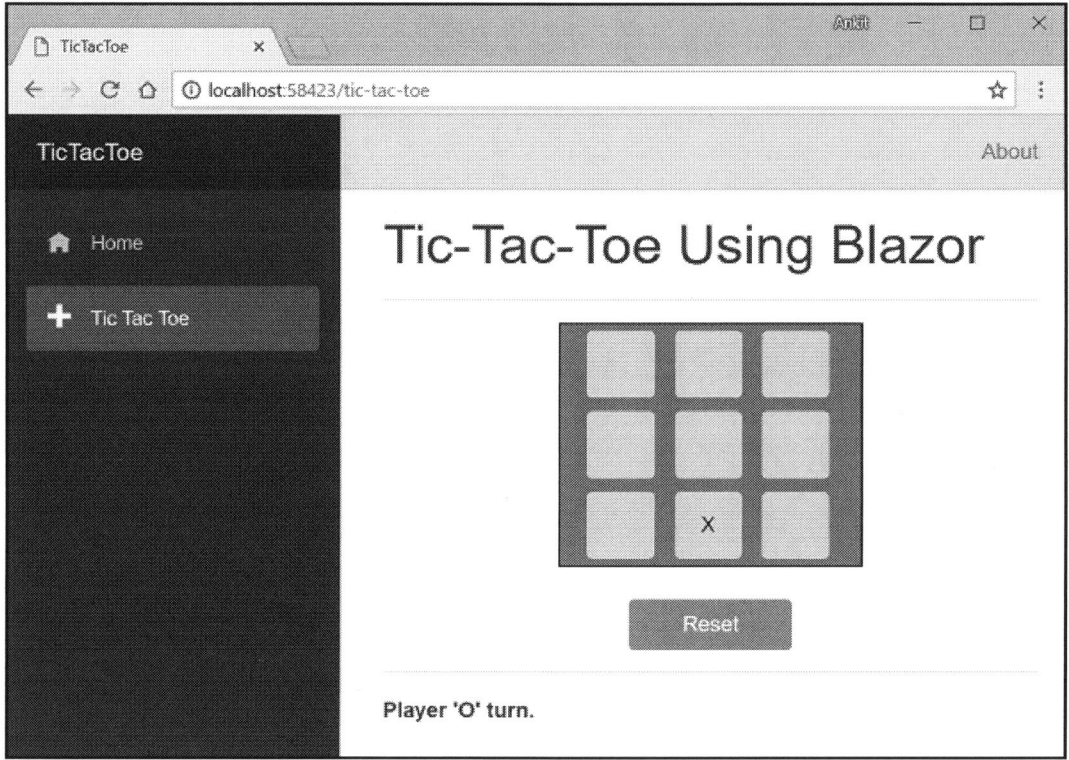

The next move will be by player **O**. So, click on any other cell and the value of the cell will be updated to **O**, as shown in the following screenshot:

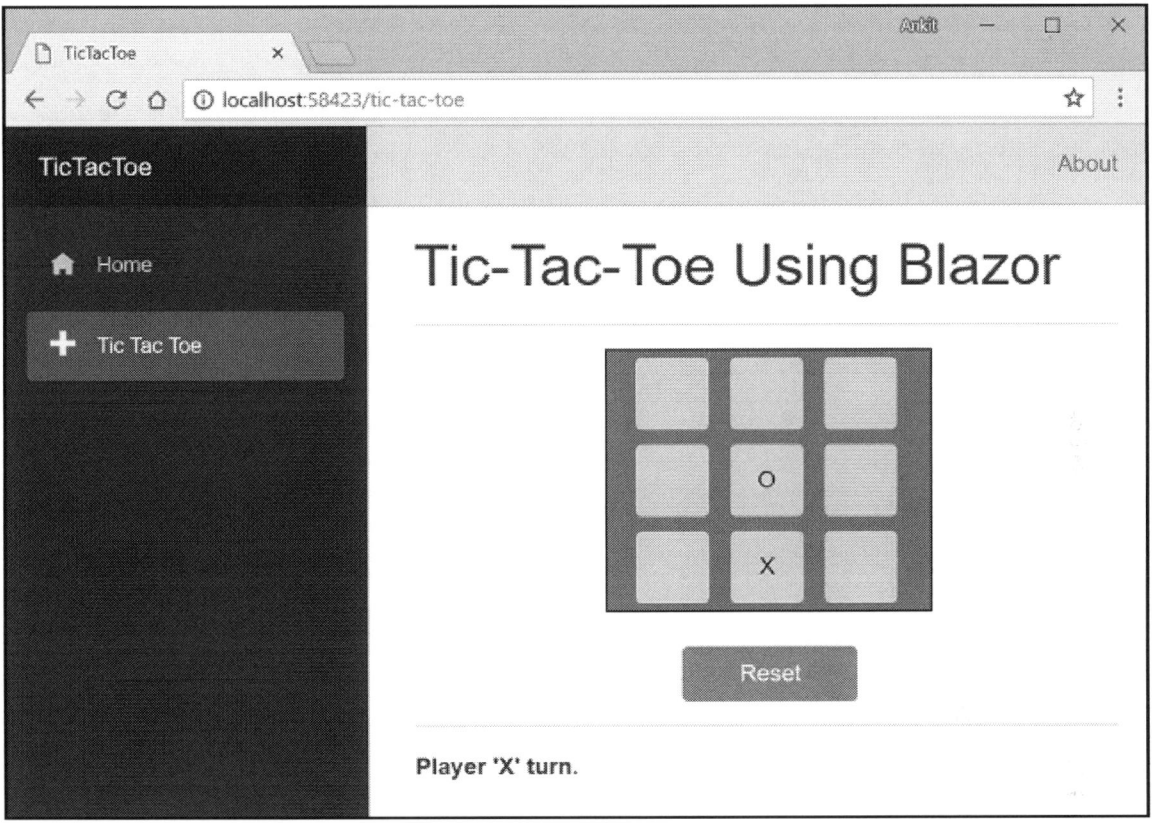

Similarly, after making a few more moves, we arrive at a win situation, where **Player 'O' has won the game**. The message will be updated showing the current winner name. Refer to the following screenshot:

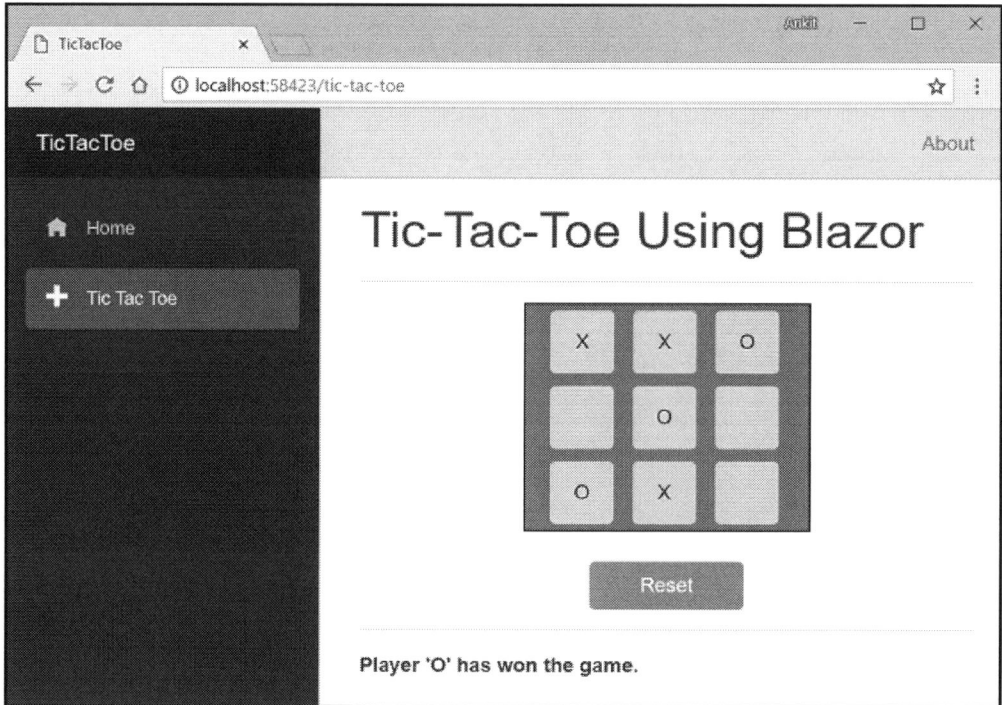

Clicking on the **Reset** button will clear the board and reset the game to its initial stage.

We will now proceed to create a basic calculator app using Blazor.

Creating a basic calculator app using Blazor

In the last section, we created a Tic-Tac-Toe game using Blazor. In this section, we will learn how to create a basic calculator app with Blazor. Since this is a basic calculator, it will take two operands, and supports four arithmetic functions—addition, subtraction, multiplication, and division. Create a client-side Blazor application in the same manner as discussed in the previous section, and name it SampleCalculator.

Creating the component

For this application, we will use the *single page component* structure. The logic and the UI will be in the same file. To create our component, right-click on `SampleCalculator/Pages` folder and then select **Add** | **New Item**. An **Add New Item** dialog box will open, asking you to select the desired item template from the provided list of items. Select **ASP.NET Core** from the left panel, and then select `Razor View` from the templates panel. Put the name of file as `Calculator.cshtml` and click **Add**. Refer to the following screenshot:

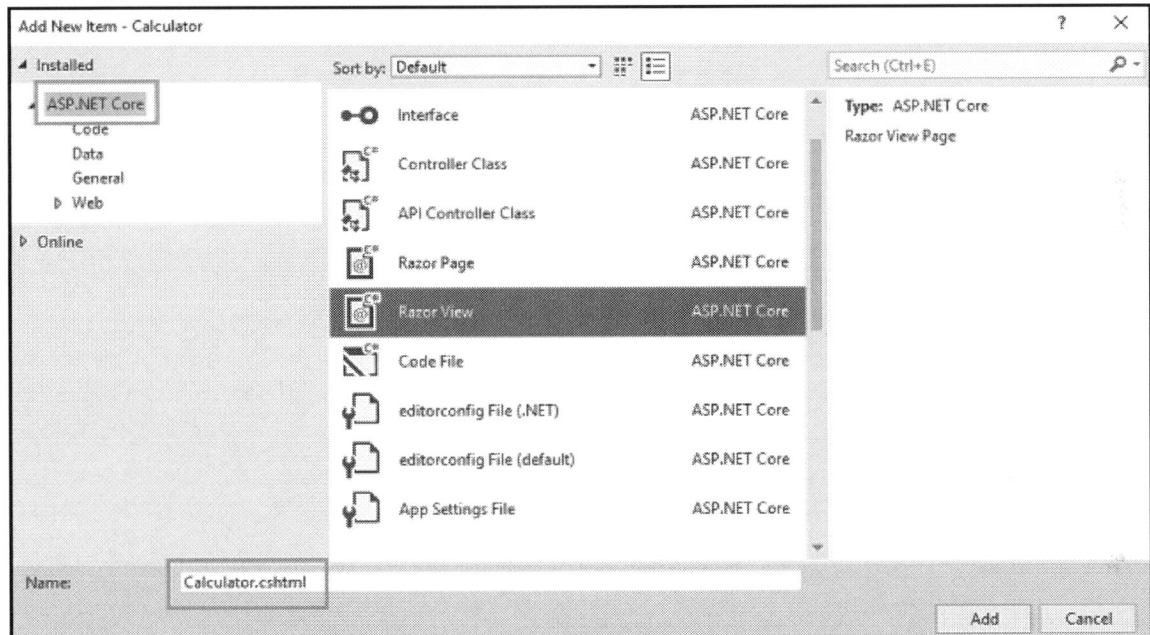

Creating the UI of the application

Open the `Calculator.cshtml` file and enter the following code into it:

```
@page "/calculator"

<h1>Basic Calculator Using Blazor</h1>
<hr />
<div>
    <div class="row">
        <div class="col-sm-3">
```

```
                <label class="control-label">First Number</label>
        </div>
        <div class="col-sm-4">
                <input class="form-control" type="text" placeholder="Enter
First Number" bind="@operand1" />
        </div>
    </div>
    <br />
    <div class="row">
        <div class="col-sm-3">
                <label class="control-label">Second Number</label>
        </div>
        <div class="col-sm-4">
                <input class="form-control" type="text" placeholder="Enter
Second Number" bind="@operand2" />
        </div>
    </div>
    <br />
    <div class="row">
        <div class="col-sm-3">
                <label class="control-label">Result</label>
        </div>
        <div class="col-sm-4">
                <input readonly class="form-control" bind="@finalResult" />
        </div>
    </div>
    <br />
    <div class="row">
        <div class="col-md-3">
                <button onclick="@AddNumbers" class="btn btn-primary">Add
(+)</button>
        </div>
        <div class="col-md-3">
                <button onclick="@SubtractNumbers" class="btn btn-
warning">Subtract (-)</button>
        </div>
        <div class="col-md-3">
                <button onclick="@MultiplyNumbers" class="btn btn-success
">Multiply (X)</button>
        </div>
        <div class="col-md-3">
                <button onclick="@DivideNumbers" class="btn btn-info">Divide
(/)</button>
        </div>
    </div>
</div>
```

In the HTML part of the code, we have defined two textboxes to read the operand input from the user, and a textbox to display the result of arithmetic operations. These textboxes will bind the value to the properties using the bind attribute. The result field is declared as `readonly`, so the user cannot edit it. We have also defined four buttons, one for each arithmetic operation. The `onclick` event of the buttons will invoke the methods that will provide the output, once it has performed the corresponding operation on both operands.

Adding the calculator logic

Finally, we will add the logic for our calculator app. Add the following code to the `Calculator.cshtml` file:

```
@functions {

double operand1 { get; set; }
double operand2 { get; set; }
string finalResult { get; set; }

void AddNumbers()
{
    finalResult = (operand1 + operand2).ToString();
}
void SubtractNumbers()
{
    finalResult = (operand1 - operand2).ToString();
}
void MultiplyNumbers()
{
    finalResult = (operand1 * operand2).ToString();
}
void DivideNumbers()
{
    if (operand2 != 0)
    {
        finalResult = (operand1 / operand2).ToString();
    }
    else
    {
        finalResult = "Cannot Divide by Zero";
    }
}
}
```

In the @functions section, we have defined two properties to bind to the user input value, and another property to display the calculation result. To handle our arithmetic operations, we have defined four methods that will perform the desired operations on the operands, and set the value of finalResult that will then bind to the Result field on the UI.

Running the application

Add the navigation link in the NavMenu.cshtml file and press *F5* to launch the application. Click on the navigation link on the menu on the left. It will open a page similar to the one shown in the following screenshot:

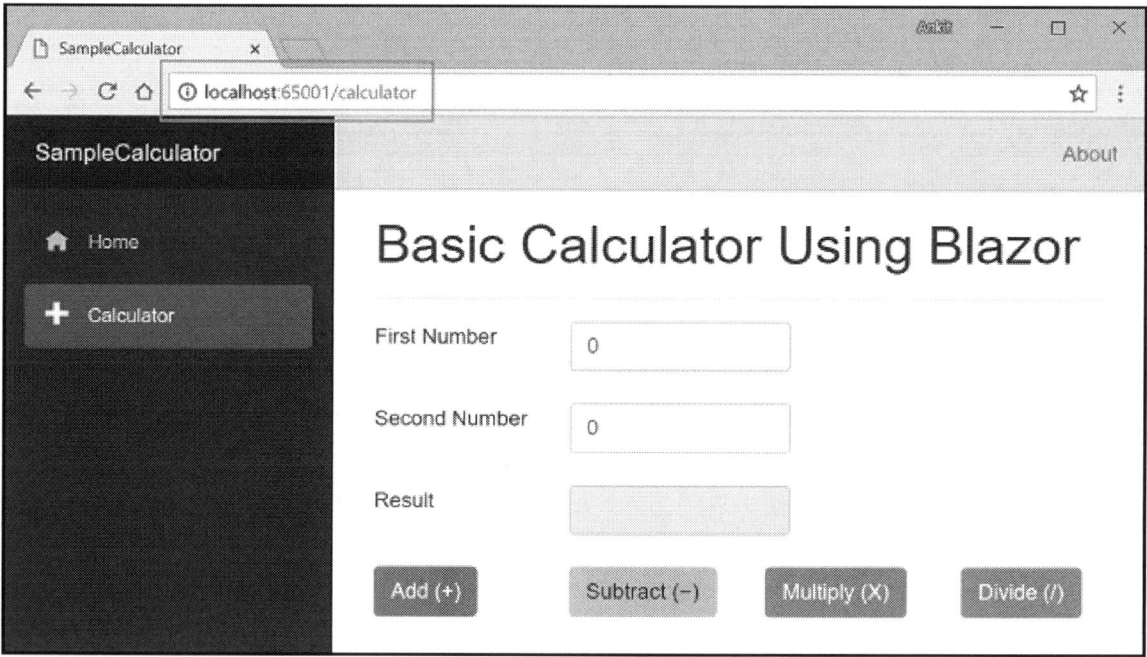

Enter two numbers and click on the button to perform any operation, and you should see the result in the results box. In the following screenshot, we perform the Add operation on two numbers and display the result:

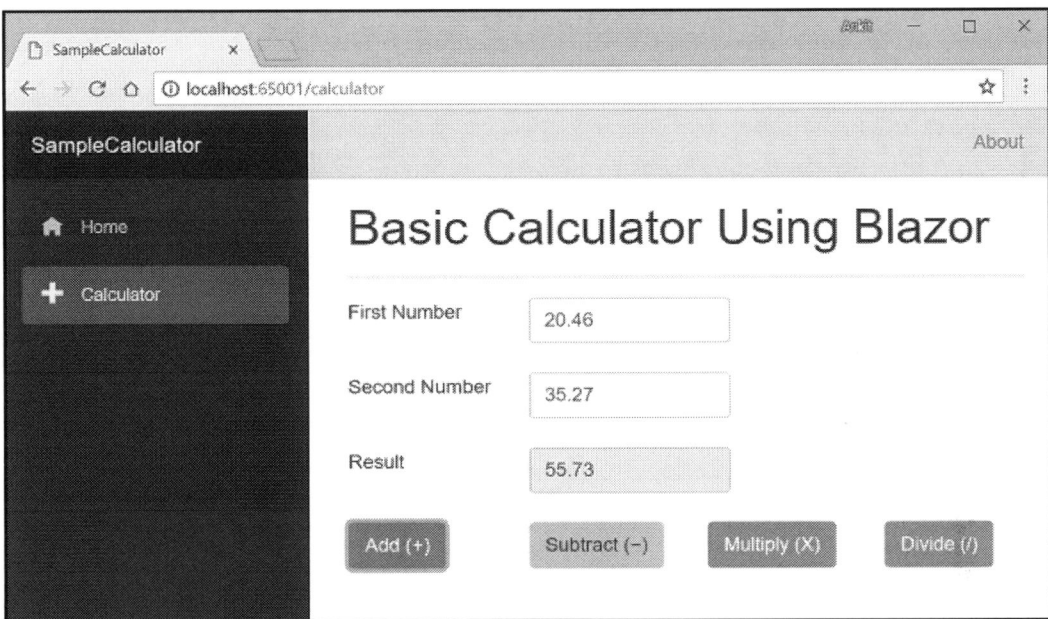

While performing a division on two numbers, if you try to perform division by zero, you will get an error message reading **Cannot Divide by Zero**. Refer to the following screenshot:

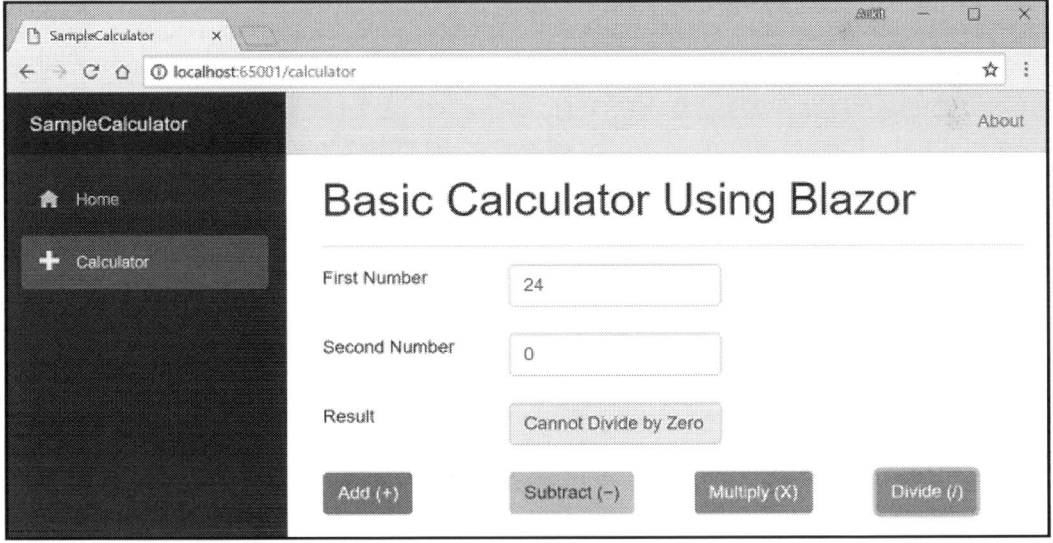

Summary

In this chapter, we learned how to create a client-side application using Blazor. We created two sample applications, a Tic-Tac-Toe game and a sample calculator app, with the help of VS 2017. We also implemented both the one-way and two-way data-binding features of the Blazor framework. These applications can run independently on the browser, without any interaction with a database.

In the next chapter, we will create a more elaborate application with database interaction, and perform CRUD operations on it.

5
Creating a Single Page Application Using Blazor

In the previous chapter, we learned how to create a client-side application using Blazor. We created two sample applications that run in the browser, without any server or database interaction. While this type of small, standalone application is great for learning and understanding the core concepts of the framework, they are rarely used in the real world. Real-world applications work on a much larger scale, with a database on the backend to store and manipulate the user data. In this chapter, we will learn how to create a **Single Page Application (SPA)** with database interaction using the Blazor framework. The server-side part of the application will be discussed in this chapter, whereas the client-side coding will be discussed in the next chapter.

We will explore the following topics in detail:

- Creating the database objects
- Creating a Blazor application using **Visual Studio (VS)** 2017
- Scaffolding the model using **Entity Framework (EF)** Core's database-first approach
- Creating a data access layer using EF Core
- Creating a data access layer using ADO.NET
- Adding the API controller to the application

We will learn two different methods for handling database interaction in a Blazor application: one using EF Core, and the other using ADO.NET.

To create our Blazor application, we will use VS 2017. We will also use Microsoft SQL Server for data storage. In this demo, I will be using SQL Server 2017, but you can use any version above SQL Server 2008. Since we already installed the Blazor Language Services extension in the previous chapter, we are ready to proceed with creating the Blazor application.

Creating the database objects

We will be using two tables to store our data:

- `Employee`: This table is used to store the records of employees. It has five fields: `EmployeeID`, `EmployeeName`, `CityName`, `Designation`, and `Gender`.
- `Cities`: This contains a list of cities, and is used to populate the `CityName` field of the Employee table. This table has two fields: `CityID` and `CityName`.

We will also create a few stored procedures to handle data manipulation. These stored procedures will be invoked from the ADO.NET code of our application.

Create a database called `EmployeeDB` in SQL Server. We will create our tables and stored procedures in this database.

Creating the table

Run the following code in SQL Server to create a table called `Employee`. The `EmployeeId` field is the primary key for this table:

```
CREATE TABLE Employee(
    EmployeeId INTEGER IDENTITY(1,1) PRIMARY KEY,
    EmployeeName VARCHAR(20) NOT NULL,
    CityName VARCHAR(20) NOT NULL,
    Designation VARCHAR(20) NOT NULL,
    Gender VARCHAR(6) NOT NULL
)
```

To create the `Cities` table, we run the following SQL command:

```
CREATE TABLE Cities (
CityID INTEGER IDENTITY(1,1) PRIMARY KEY,
CityName VARCHAR(20) NOT NULL
)
```

We will insert a few sample city names into the `Cities` table. Run the following SQL commands to do this:

```
INSERT INTO Cities VALUES('New York');
INSERT INTO Cities VALUES('Los Angeles');
INSERT INTO Cities VALUES('Chicago');
INSERT INTO Cities VALUES('Las Vegas');
INSERT INTO Cities VALUES('Miami');
```

Creating the stored procedures

We will create a few stored procedures to handle the CRUD operations on the `Employee` table, and to fetch the data from the `Cities` table.

Adding an employee record

Run the following command to create the `spAddEmployee` procedure, which will be used to add the record of a new employee to the `Employee` table:

```
CREATE PROCEDURE spAddEmployee
(
    @EmployeeName VARCHAR(20),
    @CityName VARCHAR(20),
    @Designation VARCHAR(20),
    @Gender VARCHAR(6)
)
AS
BEGIN
    INSERT INTO Employee (EmployeeName,CityName,Designation, Gender)
    VALUES (@EmployeeName,@CityName,@Designation, @Gender)
END
```

Updating an employee record

Run the following command to create the `spUpdateEmployee` procedure, which will be used to update the record of an existing employee:

```
CREATE PROCEDURE spUpdateEmployee
(
    @Id INTEGER ,
    @EmployeeName VARCHAR(20),
    @CityName VARCHAR(20),
    @Designation VARCHAR(20),
    @Gender VARCHAR(6)
)
AS
BEGIN
    UPDATE Employee
    SET EmployeeName=@EmployeeName,
    CityName=@CityName,
    Designation=@Designation,
    Gender=@Gender
    WHERE EmployeeId=@Id
END
```

Deleting an employee record

Run the following command to create the spDeleteEmployee procedure, which will be used to delete the record of an employee from the Employee table:

```
CREATE PROCEDURE spDeleteEmployee
(
    @Id INTEGER
)
AS
BEGIN
    DELETE FROM Employee
    WHERE EmployeeId=@Id
END
```

Fetching all employee records

Run the following command to create the spGetEmployeeList procedure, which will be used to fetch all employee records from Employee table:

```
CREATE PROCEDURE spGetEmployeeList
AS
BEGIN
    SELECT *
    from Employee
END
```

Fetching cities records

Run the following command to create the spGetCityList procedure, which will be used to fetch all the records from the Cities table:

```
CREATE PROCEDURE spGetCityList
AS
BEGIN
    SELECT *
    FROM Cities
END
```

We have completed the database part of this application; so, now we will proceed to create our application using VS 2017.

Creating the Blazor application using VS 2017

To create a new Blazor application, follow these steps:

1. Inside VS 2017, navigate to **File | New | Project**.
2. A **New Project** window will open. Select **.NET Core** from the panel on the left.
3. Click on the **ASP.NET Core Web Application** option in the templates panel.
4. Provide the project name, SPAWithBlazor, in the **Name** field and click **OK**.

Refer to the following screenshot:

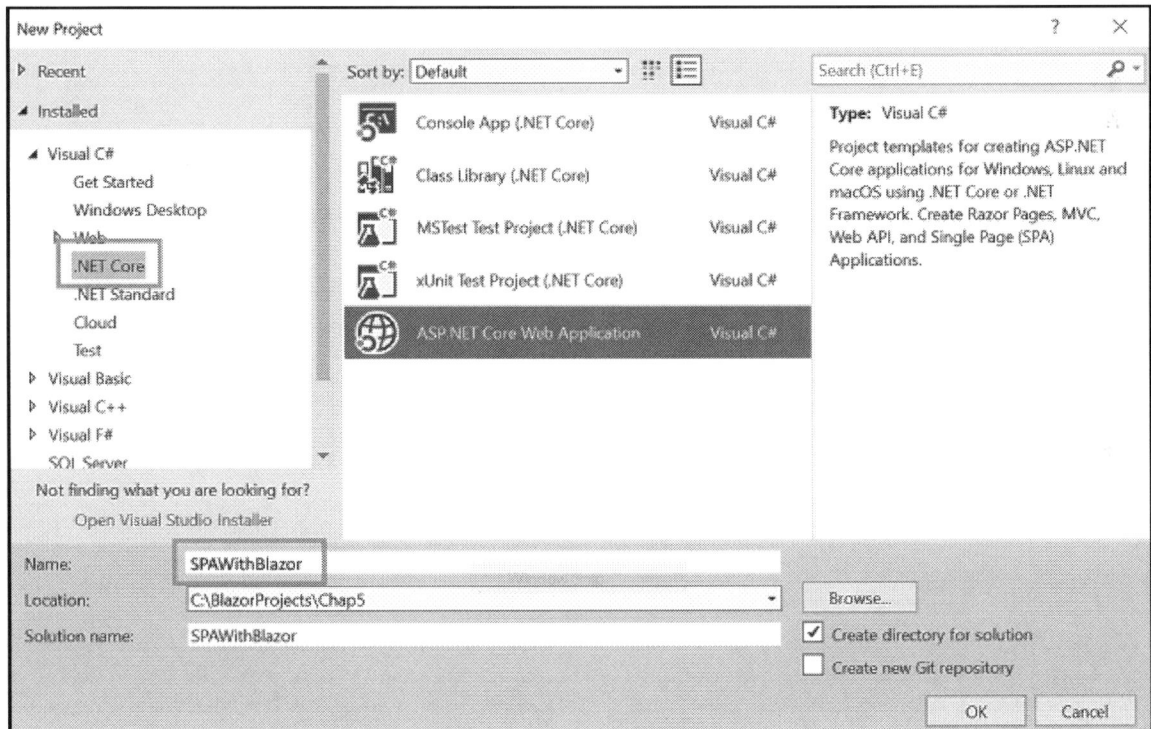

After clicking on **OK**, a new window will open. Here, you need to select the project template. Follow these steps:

1. Select **.NET Core** and **ASP.NET Core 2.1** from the drop-down menus at the top-left of the window.
2. Select **Blazor (ASP .NET Core hosted)** template from the template window and click on **OK**.

Refer to the following screenshot for a better understanding:

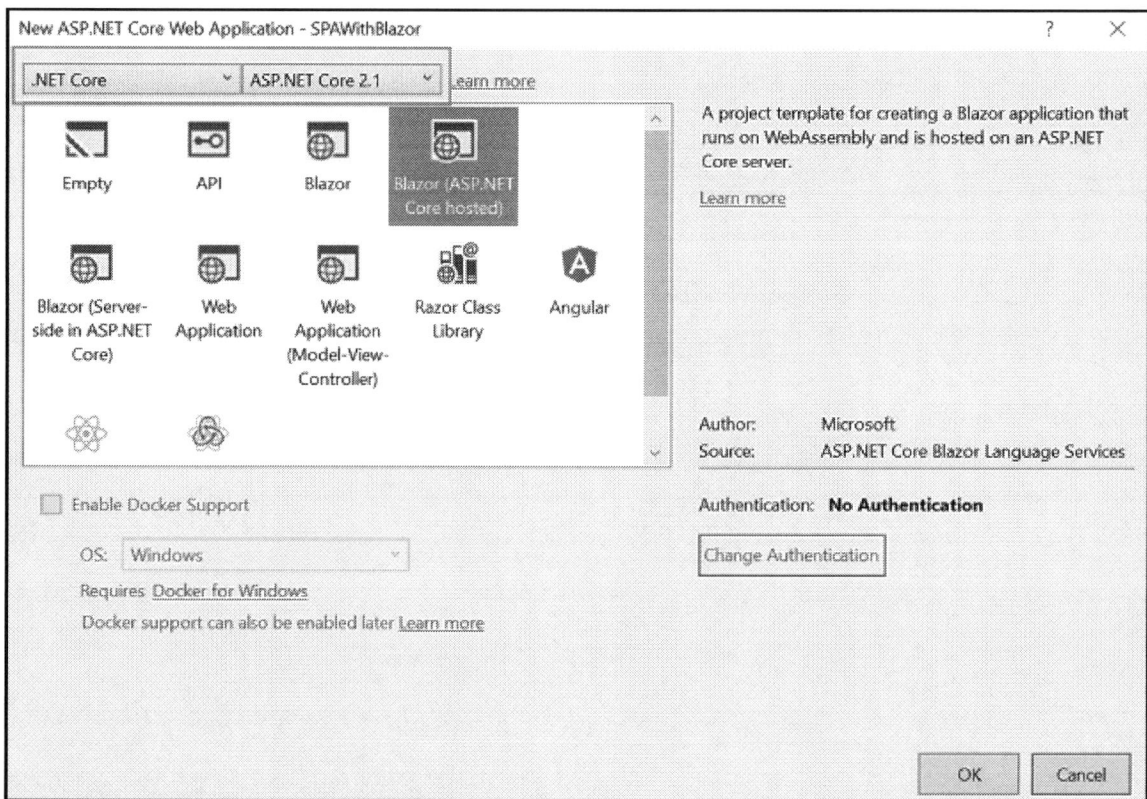

This will create our Blazor application. You can observe the folder structure of the application, as shown in the following screenshot:

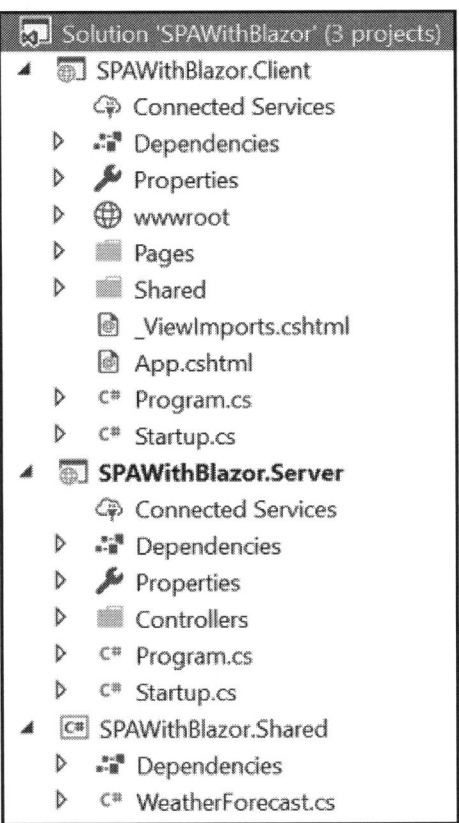

You can observe that we have created three project files in this solution:

- **SPAWithBlazor.Client**: This project contains the client-side code of the application. The Blazor components, such as view pages, will be present in this project.
- **SPAWithBlazor.Server**: This is the server-side part of our application. It contains the data access layer, the web API, and so on, which will handle the business logic of our application.
- **SPAWithBlazor.Shared**: This is a shared project. The code written in this project, which will consist of the model of our application, can be accessed by both the client and server projects.

Scaffolding the model using EF Core's database-first approach

We will scaffold our model class using EF Core's database-first approach. The model class will be created in the SPAWithBlazor.Shared project.

Navigate to **Tools | NuGet Package Manager | Package Manager Console**. Select **SPAWithBlazor.Shared** from the **Default project** drop-down menu. Refer to the following screenshot:

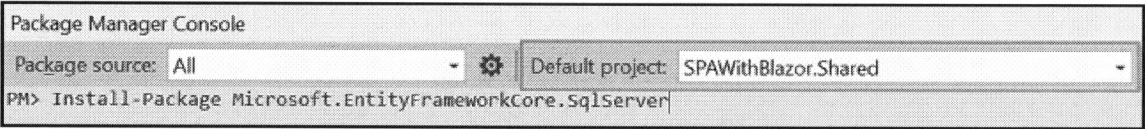

Since we are using SQL Server as our database provider, we will install the package for it. Run the following command in the Package Manager Console:

```
Install-Package Microsoft.EntityFrameworkCore.SqlServer
```

We will use EF Tools to scaffold our model classes from an existing database. Execute the following command to install the EF Core Tools package in our project:

```
Install-Package Microsoft.EntityFrameworkCore.Tools
```

Finally, run the following code to scaffold our model class:

```
Scaffold-DbContext "Data Source=SQLServer\\SQLEXPRESS;Initial
Catalog=EmployeeDB;User Id=dbuser; Password=12345;"
Microsoft.EntityFrameworkCore.SqlServer -OutputDir Models -Tables Employee,
Cities
```

In the preceding code sample, I have provided my database connection string. You will need to replace this value with your own connection string. Put the connection string value inside quotes (" ") before executing the command. Upon successful execution, a folder called **Models** will be created inside the SPAWithBlazor.Shared project. The **Models** folder should contain three class files: EmployeeDBContext.cs, Cities.cs, and Employee.cs. The name of the DBContext class will be our database name, suffixed with the word Context; hence, in our case, it is EmployeeDBContext.

Creating the data access layer for the application

Now that we have successfully created our model, we will create the data access layer, which will handle the database operations. We can access the data using either EF Core or ADO.NET from a Blazor application. We will learn about both methods in this section.

Right-click on the `SPAWithBlazor.Server` project and select **Add** | **New** folder. Name the folder `DataAccess`. We will add our data access layer class to this folder.

Data access using EF Core

Right-click on the `DataAccess` folder and select Add | Class. Name your class `DataAccessWithEF.cs`. We will use EF Core to add the methods to access the database.

Fetching all employee records

Open the `DataAccessWithEF.cs` file and add the following method definition inside the `DataAccessWithEF` class:

```
private EmployeeDBContext _employeeContext = new EmployeeDBContext();

public List<Employee> GetAllEmployees()
{
  try
  {
    return _employeeContext.Employee.ToList();
  }
  catch
  {
    throw;
  }
}
```

Here, we have created an object of our `EmployeeDBContext` class. The `GetAllEmployees` method will return the list of all the employee records present in the `Employee` table.

Adding a new employee record

Again, add the AddEmployee method definition to the class:

```
public void AddEmployee(Employee employee)
{
  try
  {
    _employeeContext.Employee.Add(employee);
    _employeeContext.SaveChanges();
  }
  catch
  {
    throw;
  }
}
```

This method will take an Employee object as a parameter and add it to the Employee table of our database.

Updating an employee record

Enter the following code to add UpdateEmployee method to the class:

```
public void UpdateEmployee(Employee employee)
{
  try
  {
    _employeeContext.Entry(employee).State = EntityState.Modified;
    _employeeContext.SaveChanges();
  }
  catch
  {
    throw;
  }
}
```

This method will take an Employee object as a parameter and update the record corresponding to the employee id of the object in the Employee table.

Fetching the records of an employee

Add the `GetEmployeeData` method definition using the following code:

```
public Employee GetEmployeeData(int id)
{
  try
  {
    Employee employee = _employeeContext.Employee.Find(id);
    return employee;
  }
  catch
  {
    throw;
  }
}
```

This method will accept the `employee id` as the parameter and return the record of the employee that corresponds to the given `employee id`.

Deleting an employee record

Add the `DeleteEmployee` method definition using the following code:

```
public void DeleteEmployee(int id)
{
  try
  {
    Employee emp = _employeeContext.Employee.Find(id);
    _employeeContext.Employee.Remove(emp);
    _employeeContext.SaveChanges();
  }
  catch
  {
    throw;
  }
}
```

This method will take `employee id` as a parameter, and perform a `delete` operation in the `Employee` table on the record that corresponds to that `employee id`.

Fetching the list of cities

Finally, add the `GetCityData` method to our class as follows:

```
public List<Cities> GetCityData()
{
  try
  {
    return _employeeContext.Cities.ToList();
  }
  catch
  {
    throw;
  }
}
```

This method will fetch the list of all the city data from the `Cities` table.

And with this, we have completed creating our data access layer using EF Core. Next, we will understand the ADO.NET approach for accessing the database.

Data access using ADO.NET

Right-click on the `DataAccess` folder and select **Add** | **Class**. Name your class `DataAccessWithADO.cs`.

Open `DataAccessWithADO.cs` and enter the following code into it:

```
using SPAWithBlazor.Shared.Models;
using System;
using System.Collections.Generic;
using System.Data;
using System.Data.SqlClient;
using System.Linq;
using System.Threading.Tasks;

namespace SPAWithBlazor.Server.DataAccess
{
    public class DataAccessWithADO
    {
        private string _connectionString = "Data
Source=SQLServer\\SQLEXPRESS;Initial Catalog=EmployeeDB;User Id=dbuser;
Password=12345;";
    }
}
```

Here, we created a `DataAccessWithADO` class and initialized the connection string for data access. You need to use your own connection string value. We will create the same six methods for data access here as we created using EF Core.

Fetching all employee records

Add the `GetAllEmployees` method definition as follows:

```
public List<Employee> GetAllEmployees()
{
  List<Employee> lstemployee = new List<Employee>();

  try
  {
    SqlConnection connection = new SqlConnection(_connectionString);
    SqlCommand cmd = new SqlCommand("spGetEmployeeList", connection);
    cmd.CommandType = CommandType.StoredProcedure;

    connection.Open();
    SqlDataAdapter sda = new SqlDataAdapter(cmd);
    DataSet dataset = new DataSet();
    sda.Fill(dataset);
    connection.Close();

    foreach (DataRow dr in dataset.Tables[0].Rows)
    {
      Employee employee = new Employee();

      employee.EmployeeId = Convert.ToInt32(dr["EmployeeID"]);
      employee.EmployeeName = dr["EmployeeName"].ToString();
      employee.CityName = dr["CityName"].ToString();
      employee.Designation = dr["Designation"].ToString();
      employee.Gender = dr["Gender"].ToString();

      lstemployee.Add(employee);
    }
  }
  catch
  {
    throw;
  }
  return lstemployee;
}
```

This method will execute the `spGetEmployeeList` stored procedure and return the list of employee records from the `Employee` table.

Adding a new employee record

Add the `AddEmployee` method definition to the class, as follows:

```
public void AddEmployee(Employee employee)
{
  try
  {
    using (SqlConnection con = new SqlConnection(_connectionString))
    {
      SqlCommand cmd = new SqlCommand("spAddEmployee", con);
      cmd.CommandType = CommandType.StoredProcedure;

      cmd.Parameters.AddWithValue("@EmployeeName", employee.EmployeeName);
      cmd.Parameters.AddWithValue("@CityName", employee.CityName);
      cmd.Parameters.AddWithValue("@Designation", employee.Designation);
      cmd.Parameters.AddWithValue("@Gender", employee.Gender);

      con.Open();
      cmd.ExecuteNonQuery();
      con.Close();
    }
  }
  catch
  {
    throw;
  }
}
```

This method will add a new employee record to the `Employee` table by executing the `spAddEmployee` stored procedure.

Updating an employee record

Add the `UpdateEmployee` method definition as follows:

```
public void UpdateEmployee(Employee employee)
{
  try
  {
    using (SqlConnection con = new SqlConnection(_connectionString))
    {
      SqlCommand cmd = new SqlCommand("spUpdateEmployee", con);
      cmd.CommandType = CommandType.StoredProcedure;

      cmd.Parameters.AddWithValue("@Id", employee.EmployeeId);
```

```
        cmd.Parameters.AddWithValue("@EmployeeName", employee.EmployeeName);
        cmd.Parameters.AddWithValue("@CityName", employee.CityName);
        cmd.Parameters.AddWithValue("@Designation", employee.Designation);
        cmd.Parameters.AddWithValue("@Gender", employee.Gender);

        con.Open();
        cmd.ExecuteNonQuery();
        con.Close();
      }
    }
    catch
    {
      throw;
    }
}
```

This method will execute the spUpdateEmployee stored procedure, updating the record of an existing employee in the Employee table.

Fetching the record of an employee

Add the following code for the GetEmployeeData method:

```
public Employee GetEmployeeData(int id)
{
  Employee employee = new Employee();

  try
  {
    using (SqlConnection con = new SqlConnection(_connectionString))
    {
      string sqlQuery = "SELECT * FROM Employee WHERE EmployeeID= " + id;
      SqlCommand cmd = new SqlCommand(sqlQuery, con);

      con.Open();
      SqlDataReader rdr = cmd.ExecuteReader();

      while (rdr.Read())
      {
        employee.EmployeeId = Convert.ToInt32(rdr["EmployeeID"]);
        employee.EmployeeName = rdr["EmployeeName"].ToString();
        employee.CityName = rdr["CityName"].ToString();
        employee.Designation = rdr["Designation"].ToString();
        employee.Gender = rdr["Gender"].ToString();
      }
    }
    return employee;
```

```
    }
    catch
    {
      throw;
    }
}
```

This method will execute a Select query to fetch the record of a particular employee that corresponds to the employee id supplied to it.

Deleting an employee record

Add the DeleteEmployee method definition as follows:

```
public void DeleteEmployee(int id)
{
  try
  {
    using (SqlConnection con = new SqlConnection(_connectionString))
    {
      SqlCommand cmd = new SqlCommand("spDeleteEmployee", con);
      cmd.CommandType = CommandType.StoredProcedure;

      cmd.Parameters.AddWithValue("@Id", id);

      con.Open();
      cmd.ExecuteNonQuery();
      con.Close();
    }
  }
  catch
  {
    throw;
  }
}
```

This method will execute the spDeleteEmployee stored procedure, allowing you to delete the employee record that corresponds to the employee id passed to the method.

Fetching the list of cities

Finally, we will add the `GetCityData` method definition to the `DataAccessWithADO` class, as follows:

```
public List<Cities> GetCityData()
{
   List<Cities> lstCities = new List<Cities>();

   try
   {
      SqlConnection connection = new SqlConnection(_connectionString);
      SqlCommand cmd = new SqlCommand("spGetCityList", connection);
      cmd.CommandType = CommandType.StoredProcedure;

      connection.Open();
      SqlDataAdapter sda = new SqlDataAdapter(cmd);
      DataSet dataset = new DataSet();
      sda.Fill(dataset);
      connection.Close();

      foreach (DataRow dr in dataset.Tables[0].Rows)
      {
         Cities city = new Cities();

         city.CityId = Convert.ToInt32(dr["CityId"]);
         city.CityName = dr["CityName"].ToString();

         lstCities.Add(city);
      }
      return lstCities;
   }
   catch
   {
      throw;
   }
}
```

This method will execute the `spGetCityList` stored procedure, fetching the list of all city data from the `Cities` table.

And with that, we have created the data access layer for our application. Although we have learned two techniques for data access, we only need to use one of them in our application.

Adding the API controller to the application

To create our API controller class, follow these steps:

1. Right-click on the `SPAWithBlazor.Server/Controllers` folder and select **Add | New Item**.
2. An **Add New Item** window will open. Select **ASP.NET Core** from the panel on the left.
3. Click on the **API Controller Class** option in the templates panel.
4. Provide the name for your class file as `EmployeeController.cs` in the **Name** field, and click on the **Add** button, as shown in the following screenshot:

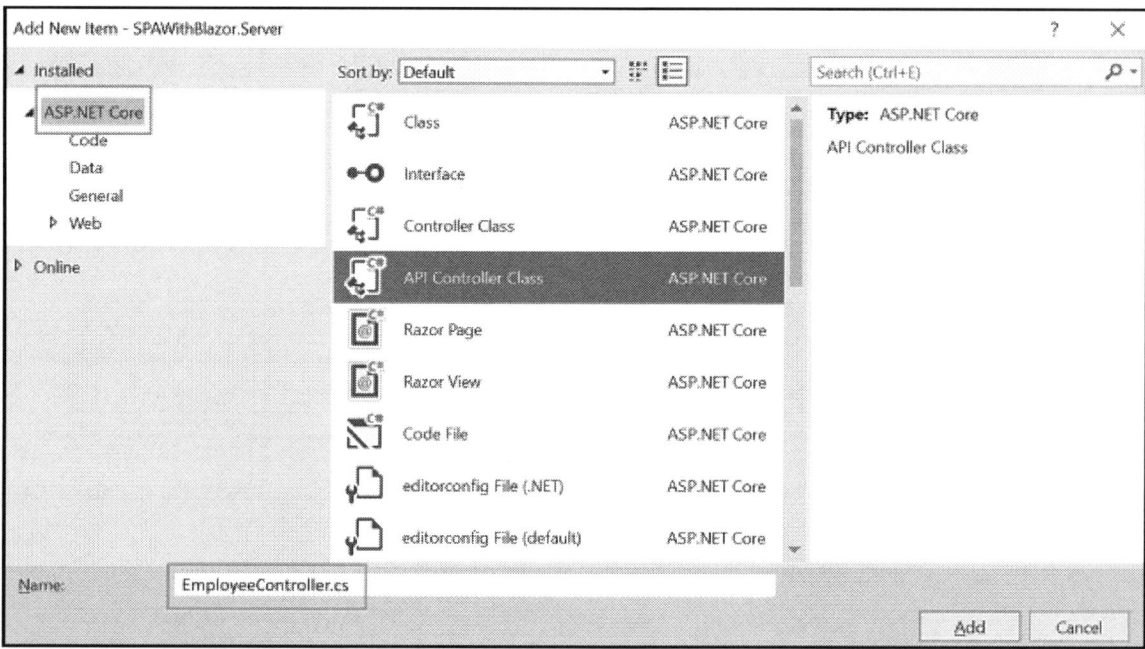

Open the `EmployeeController.cs` file and enter the following code into it:

```
using System;
using System.Collections.Generic;
using Microsoft.AspNetCore.Mvc;
using SPAWithBlazor.Server.DataAccess;
using SPAWithBlazor.Shared.Models;

namespace SPAWithBlazor.Server.Controllers
{
```

```
[Route("api/[controller]")]
public class EmployeeController : Controller
{
    DataAccessWithEF objemployee = new DataAccessWithEF();

    [HttpGet]
    public List<Employee> Get()
    {
        return objemployee.GetAllEmployees();
    }
    [HttpPost]
    public void Post([FromBody] Employee employee)
    {
        objemployee.AddEmployee(employee);
    }
    [HttpGet("{id}")]
    public Employee Get(int id)
    {
        return objemployee.GetEmployeeData(id);
    }
    [HttpPut]
    public void Put([FromBody]Employee employee)
    {
        objemployee.UpdateEmployee(employee);
    }
    [HttpDelete("{id}")]
    public void Delete(int id)
    {
        objemployee.DeleteEmployee(id);
    }
    [HttpGet("GetCities")]
    public List<Cities> GetCities()
    {
        return objemployee.GetCityData();
    }
}
}
```

At the top, we have defined Route for this API class. These APIs will be accessed by our Blazor component to manipulate the user data.

We will invoke the methods of our data access layer class from this API. Here, we invoked the methods of the DataAccessWithEF class from the API. We created an object of the DataAccessWithEF class, and then called the methods using it. If you want to use ADO.NET for data access, then you need to create an object of the DataAccessWithADO class in our API and call the methods that way.

Summary

In this chapter, we explored how can we create an ASP.NET Core-hosted Blazor application with the help of VS 2017. We also learned how to scaffold our model class using EF Core's database-first approach. Furthermore, we learned two different techniques of data access, using both EF Core and ADO.NET. We used SQL Server 2017 to handle our database. However, this application is not yet finished.

This chapter explored the server side and the business logic of our application. In the next chapter, we will continue with this application, and create the client-side part of the app and add the Blazor components to it.

6
Extending your Application

In the previous chapter, we learned how to create an ASP.NET Core-hosted Blazor application using **Visual Studio (VS)** 2017 and SQL Server. We started building a **Single Page Application (SPA)** and created an SPAWithBlazor solution file. We learned how to use an EF Core database-first approach to scaffold a model from an existing database. We also created the data access layer for the application using both the EF Core approach and the ADO.NET approach. The server side part of the application was finished in the previous chapter. Therefore, we will proceed to code our client side now.

In this chapter, we will cover the following topics:

- Creating the Blazor component
- Adding references for **JavaScript (JS)** Interop
- Adding code to the component
- Adding the navigation link for our component
- Execution demo of the application

This is an SPA, and therefore we will use a single page to handle all the CRUD operations. We will display a form in the bootstrap modal dialog. This form contains the fields for accepting employee details and a submit button. Clicking on the submit button will post the form and refresh the view to display the updated list of employees. We will bind the City field, which is a drop-down list in our form with the Cities table of the database. We are also providing a search functionality on an employee's data based on the employee name property.

We will proceed with the same solution file that we created in the previous chapter. Open the SPAWithBlazor solution with VS 2017 and create the Blazor component.

Technical requirements

You need to have knowledge on following concepts:

- C#
- ASP.NET Core
- Entity Framework Core
- Ado.NET

You should also install following software to start Blazor development.

- .NET Core 2.1 or above SDK.
- Visual Studio Code
- Visual Studio 2017 v15.7 or above
- ASP.NET Core Blazor Language Services extension

The code files of this chapter can be found on GitHub:
`https://github.com/PacktPublishing/Blazor-Quick-Start-Guide/tree/master/Chapter06/SPAWithBlazor`

Check out the following video to see the code in action:

`http://bit.ly/2SvG7Bu`

Creating the Blazor component

We will create the component file in the `SPAWithBlazor.Client/Pages` folder. The application template provides the `Counter` and `Fetch Data` files by default in this folder. Before adding our own component file, we will delete these two default files to make our solution cleaner.

To create the Blazor component, follow these steps:

1. Right-click on the `SPAWithBlazor.Client/Pages` folder and select **Add | New**.
2. An **Add New Item** window will open. Select **ASP.NET Core** from the panel on the left.
3. Click on the **Razor Page** option in the templates panel.
4. Provide the name of the component as `EmployeeData.cshtml` in the **Name** field. Click **OK**.

Refer to the following screenshot:

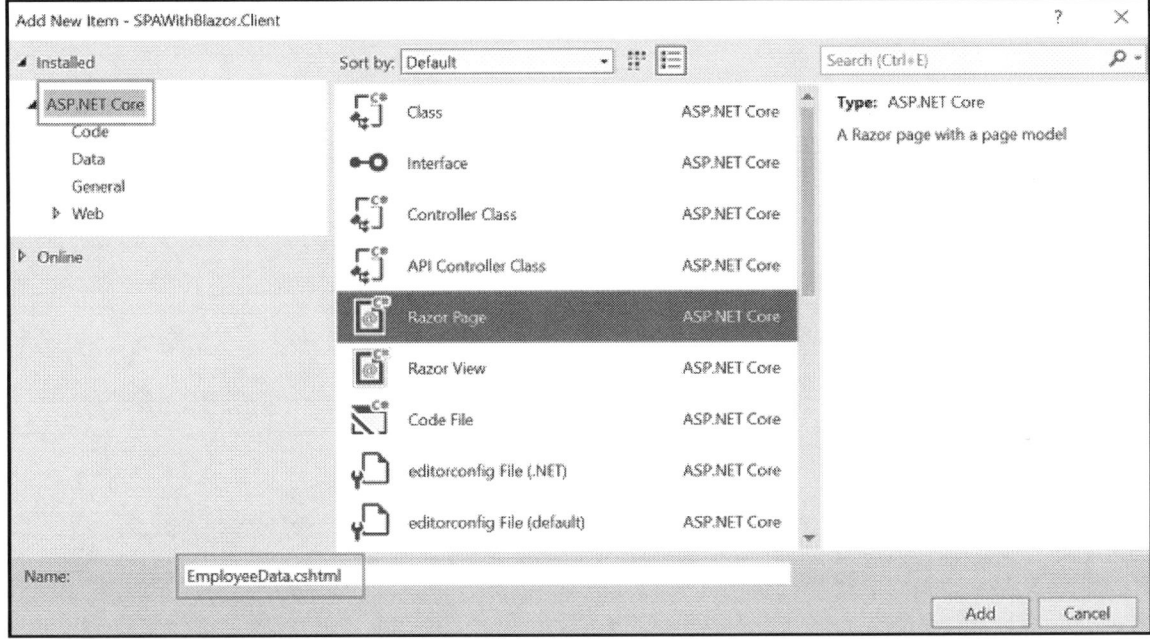

This will create our `EmployeeData` component. This component has two files:

- `EmployeeData.cshtml`: This is the view page, and it contains the HTML part of the component.
- `EmployeeData.cshtml.cs`: This is the code behind the page of our component, and it will contain the logic to make web API calls and bind the data to the view page.

Adding references for JS Interop

We will be using a bootstrap modal dialog in our application. We will also include a few Font Awesome icons for styling in the application. To be able to use these two libraries, we need to add the CDN references to allow the JS interop.

Open the `SPAWithBlazor.Client/wwwroot/index.html` file and put the following code in the `<head>` section:

```html
<link rel="stylesheet"
href="https://cdnjs.cloudflare.com/ajax/libs/font-awesome/4.7.0/css/font-aw
esome.min.css">
<script
src="https://ajax.googleapis.com/ajax/libs/jquery/3.3.1/jquery.min.js"></sc
ript>
<script
src="https://cdnjs.cloudflare.com/ajax/libs/popper.js/1.14.3/umd/popper.min
.js"></script>
<script
src="https://maxcdn.bootstrapcdn.com/bootstrap/4.1.3/js/bootstrap.min.js"><
/script>
```

Here, we have included the CDN references, which will allow us to use the bootstrap modal dialog and Font Awesome icons in our applications.

Adding code to the component

We will add the code to our component files. First, we will code the **code behind** file and then the view file.

Coding the EmployeeData.cshtml.cs file

This is the **code behind** file of our component. Open the `EmployeeData.cshtml.cs` file and put the following code into it:

```csharp
using Microsoft.AspNetCore.Blazor;
using Microsoft.AspNetCore.Blazor.Components;
using SPAWithBlazor.Shared.Models;
using System;
using System.Collections.Generic;
using System.Linq;
using System.Net.Http;
using System.Threading.Tasks;

namespace SPAWithBlazor.Client.Pages
{
    public class EmployeeDataModel : BlazorComponent
    {
        [Inject]
```

```
        protected HttpClient Http { get; set; }

        protected List<Employee> empList = new List<Employee>();
        protected List<Cities> cityList = new List<Cities>();
        protected Employee emp = new Employee();
        protected string modalTitle { get; set; }
        protected string searchString { get; set; }
    }
}
```

Here, we have defined the EmployeeDataModel class, which is inheriting from BlazorComponent. This allows the EmployeeDataModel class to act as a Blazor component.

We are also injecting the HttpClient service to enable the web API calls to our EmployeeController API.

We will use the two empList and cityList variables to hold the data of our Employee and Cities database tables respectively. The modalTitle property, which is of type string, is used to hold the title that will be displayed in the modal dialog. The value provided in the search box is stored in the searchString, property which is also of type string.

Add the following method definitions to the EmployeeDataModel class:

```
protected override async Task OnInitAsync()
{
  await GetCityList();
  await GetEmployeeList();
}
protected async Task GetCityList()
{
  cityList = await
Http.GetJsonAsync<List<Cities>>("api/Employee/GetCities");
}

protected async Task GetEmployeeList()
{
  empList = await Http.GetJsonAsync<List<Employee>>("api/Employee");
}
```

The GetCityList method will make a call to our web API GetCities method to fetch the list of city data from the Cities table. The GetEmployeeList method will send a GET request to our web API to fetch the list of Employee Data from the Employee table. We are invoking these two methods inside the OnInitAsync method, to ensure that the Employee Data and the cities data will be available as the page loads.

Add the following method definitions to the EmployeeDataModel class:

```
protected void AddEmployee()
{
  emp = new Employee();
  this.modalTitle = "Add Employee";
}
protected async Task EditEmployee(int empID)
{
  emp = await Http.GetJsonAsync<Employee>("/api/Employee/" + empID);
  this.modalTitle = "Edit Employee";
}
protected async Task SaveEmployee()
{
  if (emp.EmployeeId != 0)
  {
    await Http.SendJsonAsync(HttpMethod.Put, "api/Employee/", emp);
  }
  else
  {
    await Http.SendJsonAsync(HttpMethod.Post, "/api/Employee/", emp);
  }
  await GetEmployeeList();
}
```

The AddEmployee method will initialize an empty instance of the Employee object and set the modalTitle property, which will display the title message on the **Add modal** popup.

The EditEmployee method will accept the employee ID as the parameter. It will send a GET request to our web API to fetch the record of the employee corresponding to the employee ID passed to it.

We will use the SaveEmployee method to save the record of the employee for both the Add request and Edit request. To differentiate between the Add and the Edit requests, we will use the EmployeeId property of the Employee object. If an Edit request is made, then the EmployeeId property contains a non-zero positive value, and we will send a PUT request to our web API, which will update the record of the employee.

Otherwise, if we make an Add request, then the EmployeeId property is not initialized, and hence it is set to zero. In this case, we need to send a POST request to our web API, which will create a new employee record.

Finally, add the following method definitions to the EmployeeDataModel class:

```
protected async Task DeleteConfirm(int empID)
{
  emp = await Http.GetJsonAsync<Employee>("/api/Employee/" + empID);
}
protected async Task DeleteEmployee(int empID)
{
  await Http.DeleteAsync("api/Employee/" + empID);
  await GetEmployeeList();
}
protected async Task SearchEmployee()
{
  await GetEmployeeList();
  if (searchString != "")
  {
    empList = empList.Where(
      x => x.EmployeeName.IndexOf(searchString,
StringComparison.OrdinalIgnoreCase) != -1).ToList();
  }
}
```

The DeleteConfirm method will accept the employee ID as the parameter. It will fetch the Employee Data corresponding to the employee ID supplied to it.

The DeleteEmployee method will send a delete request to our API and pass the employee ID as the parameter. It will then call the GetEmployeeList method to refresh the view with the updated list of Employee Data.

The SearchEmployee method is used to implement the search by the employee name functionality. We will return all the records of the employee, which will match the search criteria either fully or partially. To make the search more effective, we will ignore the text case of the search string. This means the search result will be same whether the search text is in uppercase or in lowercase.

Coding the EmployeeData.cshtml file

Open the `EmployeeData.cshtml` file and put the following code into it:

```
@page "/employeerecords"
@inherits EmployeeDataModel

<h1>Employee Data</h1>

<div class="container">
    <div class="row">
        <div class="col-xs-3">
            <button class="btn btn-primary" data-toggle="modal" data-
target="#AddEditEmpModal" onclick="@AddEmployee">
                <i class="fa fa-user-plus"></i>
                Add Employee
            </button>
        </div>
        <div class="input-group col-md-4 offset-md-5">
            <input type="text" class="form-control" placeholder="Search
Employee" bind="@searchString" />
            <div class="input-group-append">
                <button class="btn btn-info" onclick="@SearchEmployee">
                    <i class="fa fa-search"></i>
                </button>
            </div>
        </div>
    </div>
</div>
<br />
```

The route for our component is defined at the top as `/employeerecords`. To use the methods defined in the `EmployeeDataModel` class, we will inherit it using the `@inherits` directive.

We have defined an `Add Employee` button. Upon clicking, this button will invoke the `AddEmployee` method and open a modal dialog, which allows the user to fill out the new `Employee Data` in a form.

We have also defined our search box and a corresponding search button. The search box will bind the value to `searchString` property. On clicking the search button, `SearchEmployee` method will be invoked, which will return the filtered list of data as per the search text.

Now, add the following lines of code to the file:

```
@if (empList == null)
{
    <p><em>Loading...</em></p>
}
else
{
    <table class='table'>
        <thead>
            <tr>
                <th>Id</th>
                <th>Name</th>
                <th>Gender</th>
                <th>Designation</th>
                <th>City</th>
            </tr>
        </thead>
        <tbody>
            @foreach (var emp in empList)
            {
                <tr>
                    <td>@emp.EmployeeId</td>
                    <td>@emp.EmployeeName</td>
                    <td>@emp.Gender</td>
                    <td>@emp.Designation</td>
                    <td>@emp.CityName</td>
                    <td>
                        <button class="btn btn-outline-dark" data-
toggle="modal" data-target="#AddEditEmpModal"
                                onclick="@(async () => await
EditEmployee(@emp.EmployeeId))">
                            <i class="fa fa-pencil-square-o"></i>
                            Edit
                        </button>
                        <button class="btn btn-outline-danger" data-
toggle="modal" data-target="#deleteEmpModal"
                                onclick="@(async () => await
DeleteConfirm(@emp.EmployeeId))">
                            <i class="fa fa-trash-o"></i>
                            Delete
                        </button>
                    </td>
                </tr>
            }
        </tbody>
    </table>
}
```

If the `empList` property is not `null`, we will bind the `Employee Data` to a table to display it on the web page. Each employee record has the following two action buttons corresponding to it:

- **Edit**: This button will perform two tasks. It will invoke the `EditEmployee` method and open the edit employee modal dialog for editing the employee record.
- **Delete**: This button will also perform two tasks. It will invoke the `DeleteConfirm` method and open a delete confirm modal dialog, asking the user to confirm the deletion of the employee's record.

Again, add the following code to this file:

```
<div class="modal fade" id="AddEditEmpModal">
    <div class="modal-dialog">
        <div class="modal-content">
            <div class="modal-header">
                <h3 class="modal-title">@modalTitle</h3>
                <button type="button" class="close" data-dismiss="modal">
                    <span aria-hidden="true">X</span>
                </button>
            </div>
            <div class="modal-body">
                <form>
                    <div class="form-group">
                        <label class="control-label">Name</label>
                        <input class="form-control"
bind="@emp.EmployeeName" />
                    </div>
                    <div class="form-group">
                        <label class="control-label">Gender</label>
                        <select class="form-control" bind="@emp.Gender">
                            <option value="">-- Select Gender --</option>
                            <option value="Male">Male</option>
                            <option value="Female">Female</option>
                        </select>
                    </div>
                    <div class="form-group">
                        <label class="control-label">Designation</label>
                        <input class="form-control" bind="@emp.Designation"
/>
                    </div>
                    <div class="form-group">
                        <label class="control-label">City</label>
                        <select class="form-control" bind="@emp.CityName">
                            <option value="">-- Select City --</option>
```

```
                              @foreach (var city in cityList)
                              {
                                  <option
value="@city.CityName">@city.CityName</option>
                              }
                         </select>
                    </div>
                </form>
            </div>
            <div class="modal-footer">
                <button class="btn btn-block btn-success"
                        onclick="@(async () => await SaveEmployee())" data-
dismiss="modal">
                    Save
                </button>
            </div>
        </div>
    </div>
</div>
```

Here, we are defining a bootstrap modal popup. We are defining a form inside the modal to accept user inputs for the employee records. The input fields of this form will bind to the properties of the employee class. The City field is a drop-down list, which will bind to the Cities table of the database with the help of the cityList variable. When we click on the save button, the SaveEmployee method will be invoked and the modal dialog will be closed.

Finally, include the following code to complete the view part of our component:

```
<div class="modal fade" id="deleteEmpModal">
    <div class="modal-dialog">
        <div class="modal-content">
            <div class="modal-header">
                <h3 class="modal-title">Confirm Delete !!!</h3>
                <button type="button" class="close" data-dismiss="modal">
                    <span aria-hidden="true">X</span>
                </button>
            </div>
            <div class="modal-body">
                <table class="table">
                    <tr>
                        <td>Name</td>
                        <td>@emp.EmployeeName</td>
                    </tr>
                    <tr>
                        <td>Gender</td>
                        <td>@emp.Gender</td>
```

```
            </tr>
            <tr>
                <td>Designation</td>
                <td>@emp.Designation</td>
            </tr>
            <tr>
                <td>City</td>
                <td>@emp.CityName</td>
            </tr>
        </table>
    </div>
    <div class="modal-footer">
        <button class="btn btn-danger" data-dismiss="modal"
                onclick="@(async () => await
DeleteEmployee(emp.EmployeeId))">
            Delete
        </button>
        <button data-dismiss="modal" class="btn">Cancel</button>
    </div>
</div>
</div>
</div>
```

Here, we are defining a bootstrap modal dialog, which will be displayed when the user clicks on the Delete button corresponding to an employee record. This modal will show the Employee Data in a table and ask the user to confirm the deletion. Clicking on the **Delete** button inside this modal dialog will invoke the DeleteEmployee method and close the modal. Clicking on the **Cancel** button will close the modal without performing any action on the data.

Adding the navigation link to our component

Before executing the application, we will add the navigation link to our component in the navigation menu.

Open the SPAWithBlazor.Client/Shared/NavMenu.cshtml page and add the following navigation link:

```
<li class="nav-item px-3">
  <NavLink class="nav-link" href="employeerecords">
    <span class="oi oi-list-rich" aria-hidden="true"></span> Employee Data
  </NavLink>
</li>
```

Here, we are adding a new menu item—Employee Data—in the navigation menu. Upon clicking this link, the user will be redirected to the EmployeeData component, and the route for this component—/employeerecords—will be appended to the URL.

Execution demo

Press *F5* to launch the application.

It will open a web page as shown in the following screenshot. The navigation menu on the left is showing the navigation link for the **Employee Data** page:

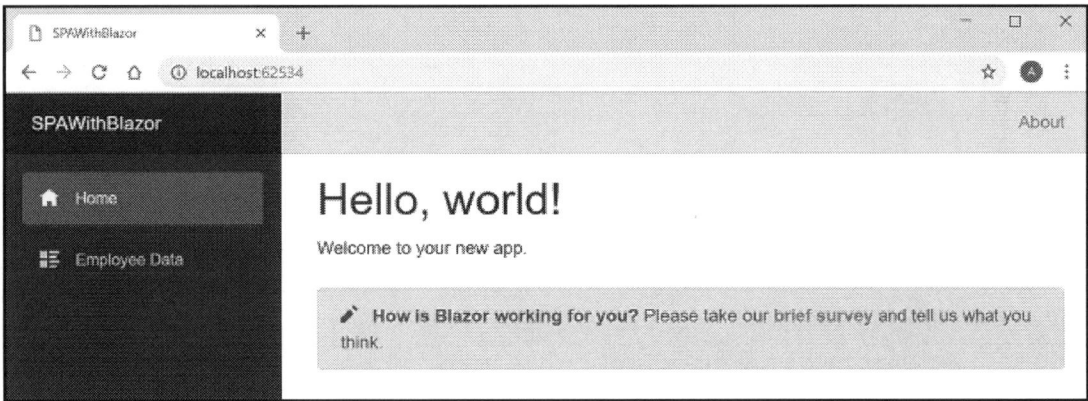

Clicking on the **Employee Data** link in the navigation menu will take you to the **Employee Data** view. This is currently showing an empty table, as we have not added any employee records. Notice that the URL has /employeerecords appended to it:

To add a new employee record, we need to click on the **Add Employee** button. It will open an **Add Employee** modal popup, which contains a form with the input fields for entering values for employee data. Put values in all the fields and click on **Save** to create a new employee record.

Take a look at this screenshot:

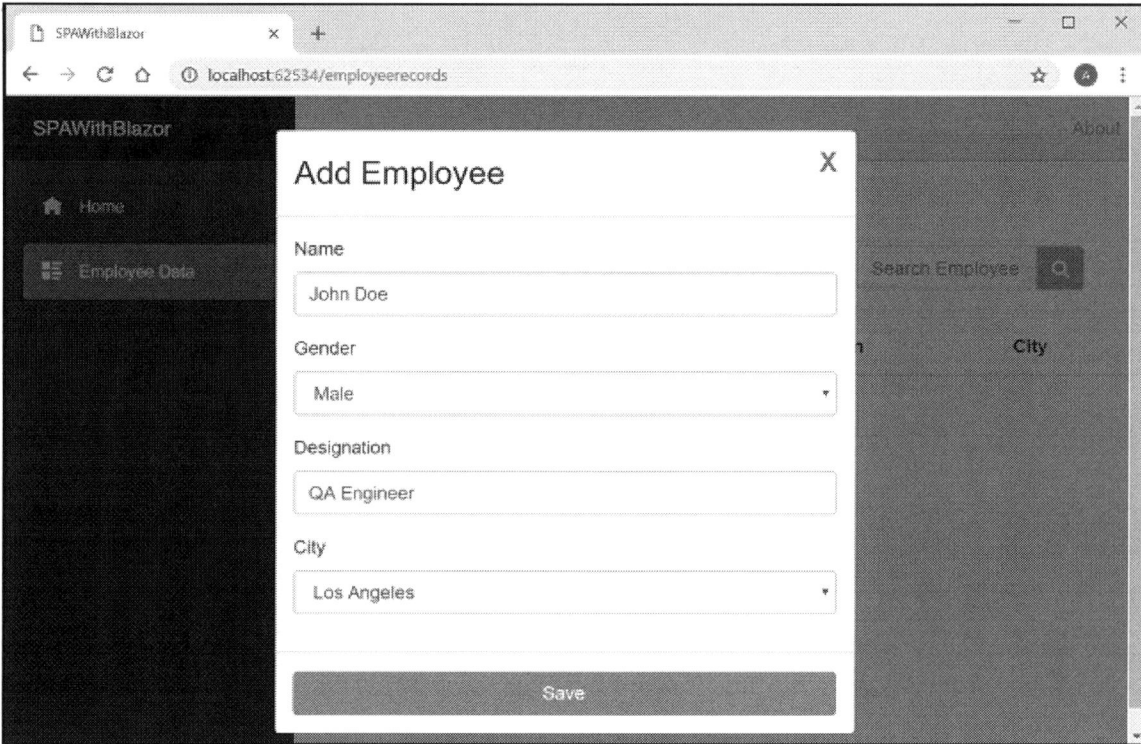

Once we click on the **Save** button, the modal popup will be closed. The view will be refreshed and the newly added employee data will be displayed in the table. After adding a few records, the view will look similar to the one shown here:

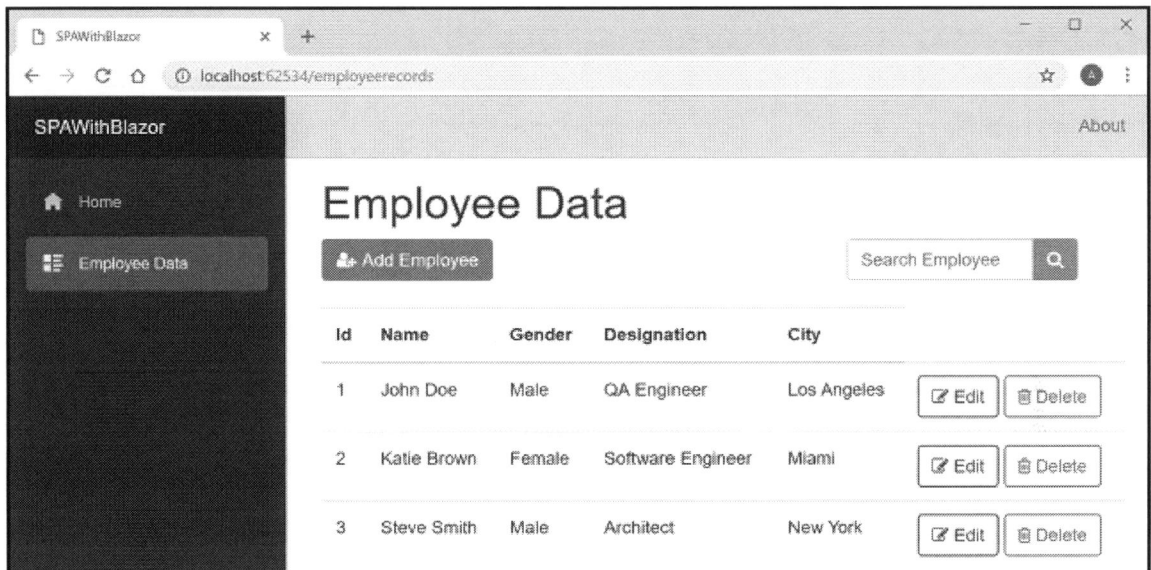

Here, you will observe two action buttons corresponding to each employee record. If we click on the **Edit** button, it will open the modal popup for editing the employee record. The input fields of the form will already contain the existing employee data, and we can change the values as we want to edit it. Clicking on **Save** will update the records and refresh the view to display the record.

Refer to this screenshot:

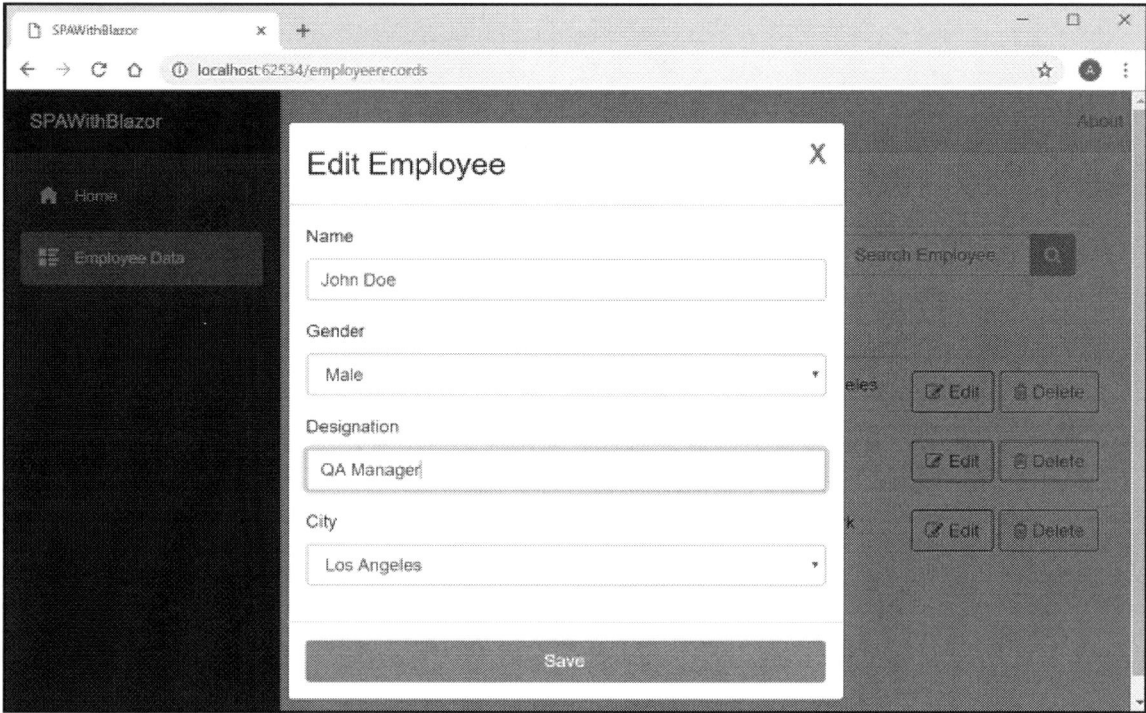

To search for an employee data, enter the employee name in the search box and click on search button. It will return all the records matching the search text. The search text is also case independent. If we perform an empty search then it will display all the records in the table .

Refer to the screenshot below:

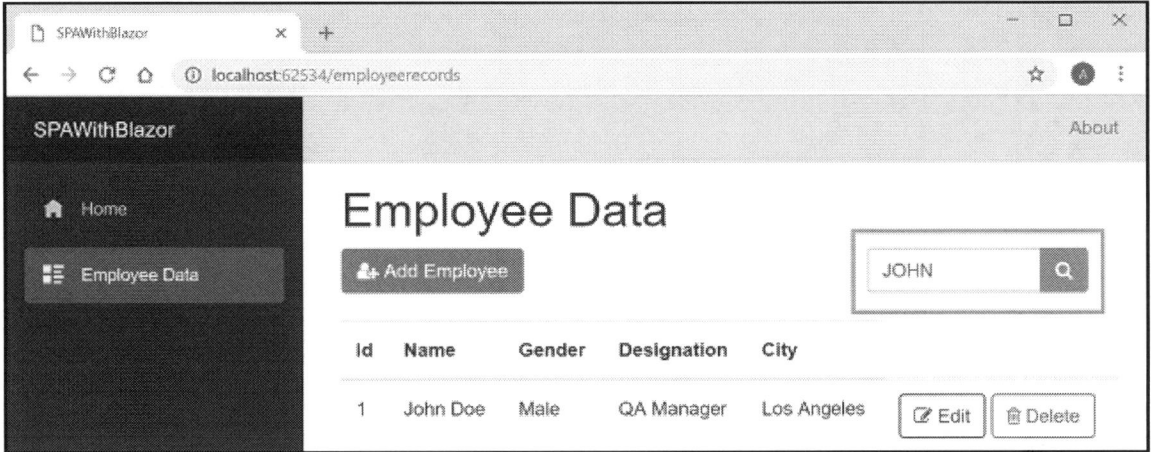

Clicking on the **Delete** action button in the table will open a **Confirm Delete !!!** modal. This will display the employee data in a table asking for the confirmation to delete this record. Clicking on the **Delete** button in this modal will delete the employee record, close the popup, and refresh the view to display the updated set of employee records:

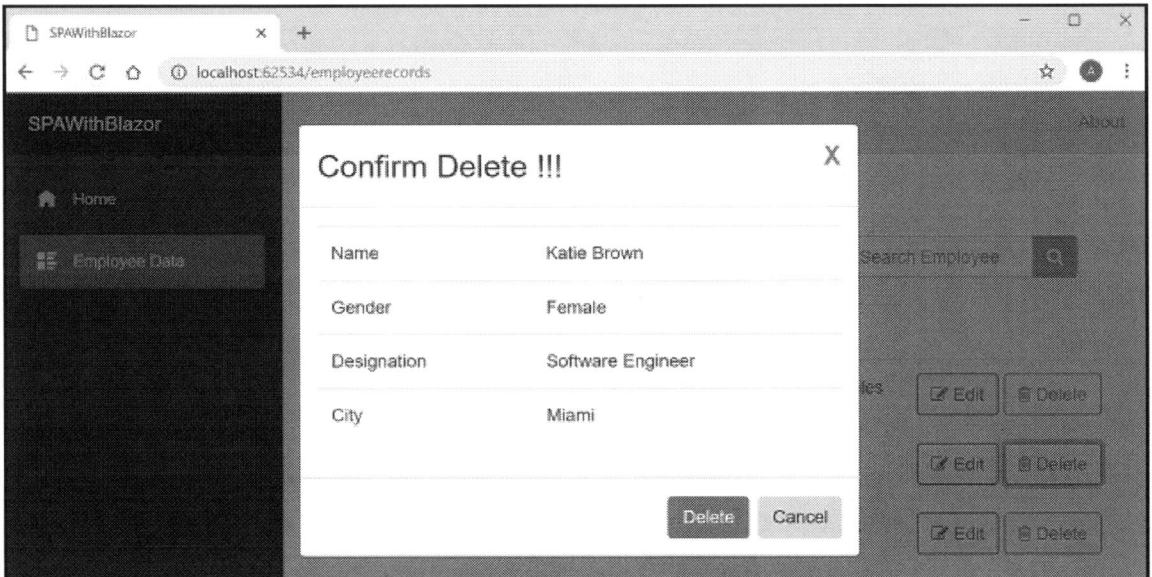

Summary

In this chapter, we finished the ASP.NET Core-hosted Blazor application that we started in the previous chapter. We created the Blazor component and completed the client side of our application. We learned how to call web API methods from the Blazor component and bind the data to an HTML DOM. We also executed the application and performed the CRUD operations on it.

In the next chapter, we will understand how we can host this application on IIS and on Azure cloud.

7
Hosting and Deployment

In the last two chapters, we learned how to create an ASP.NET core hosted Blazor application. We understood how to use EF core and ADO.NET for database connectivity to a Blazor application. We also learned to invoke the web API methods from the Blazor client-side code and bind it to HTML elements. However, the application we created is still in a development environment, and to expose it to the world, we need to host the application and publish it.

In this chapter, we are going to learn how we can deploy a Blazor application. We will explore the following two deployment techniques:

- Deploying a Blazor app on IIS
- Deploying a Blazor app on Azure

We will deploy the `SPAWithBlazor` application that we created in the previous chapter.

Deploying a Blazor app on IIS

We will deploy our SPAWithBlazor application on IIS to our local machine. We will use IIS 10 and Visual Studio 2017 on a Windows 10 machine for this demo.

Prerequisites

Before hosting the Blazor app on IIS, we need to install a few applications on our machine. Make sure you fulfill the following prerequisites.

Installing IIS

The first step is to install IIS on your machine.

Navigate to **Control Panel** | **Programs and Features** | **turn the Windows feature on or off**. It will open a window showing all the installed Windows features of your machine. Select the Internet Information Services option and click OK.

Internet Information Services (IIS) will be installed on your machine. If you are prompted to restart your machine, then restart it and proceed to the next step.

Installing the URL rewrite module

The URL rewrite module allows us to create URL rules that are easier for users to remember and are search-engine friendly. It also gives us control over the application URL redirection and responses based on the rewrite rule logic.

It also enables IIS to parse the web.config file. If this module is missing, then IIS cannot read the web.config file and the website will not load.

Open `https://www.iis.net/downloads/microsoft/url-rewrite` and install the URL rewrite module in your machine.

Installing .NET Core hosting bundle

Since we are installing an ASP.NET core hosted application, we need to install the .NET Core hosting bundle on our machine.

Follow the steps mentioned here:

1. Navigate to `https://www.microsoft.com/net/download`.
2. Click on the **Download .NET Core Runtime** button under **.NET Core** section on the page. It will download a dotnet-hosting executable file:

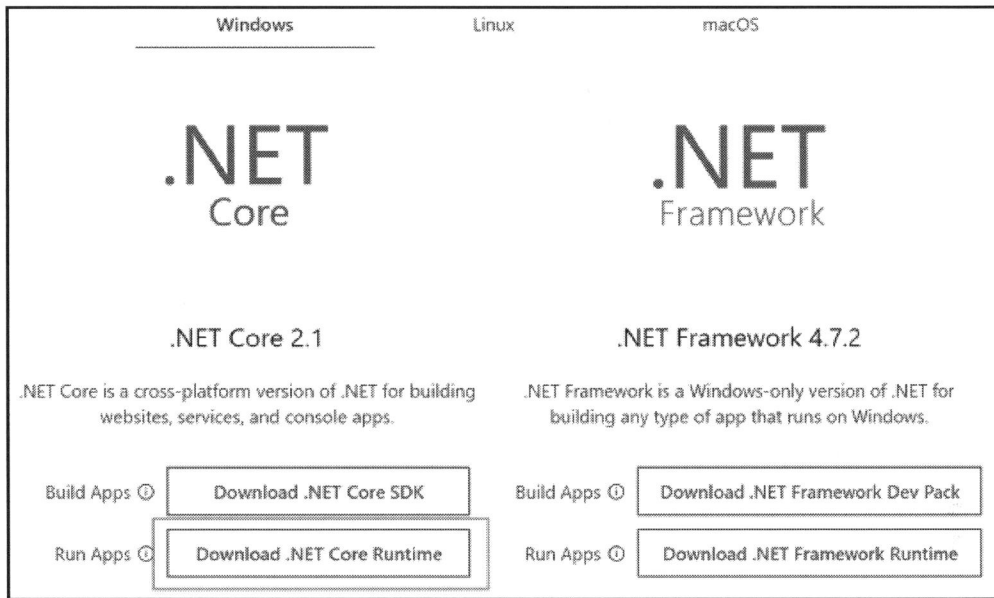

3. Once the download is finished, double-click on the dotnet-hosting executable file to start installing it. You will see a window similar to this one:

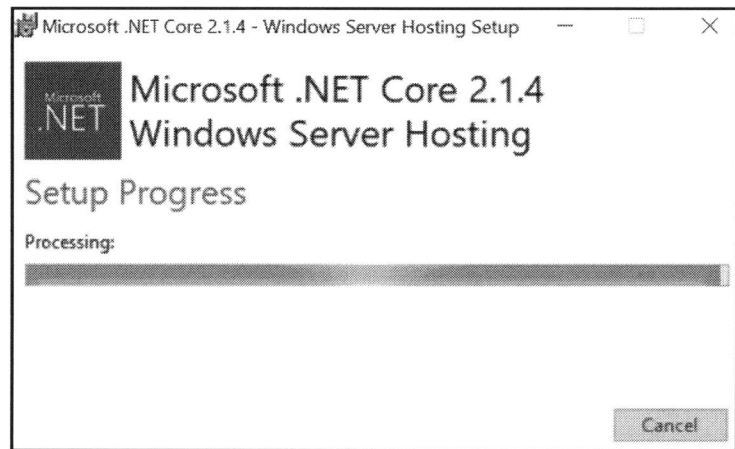

Once the installation is finished, your machine is ready to host a Blazor application on IIS.

Following are the steps to ensure the installation is completed:

1. Install the .NET Core hosting bundle after installing IIS only. This is to ensure that the .NET core hosting bundle will install dependencies for IIS as well.
2. Restart your machine once you have installed the .NET Core hosting bundle. This ensures that the IIS will take an updated reference of the system PATH variable, which is changed by installing the .NET Core hosting bundle

Publishing the Blazor app to IIS

After all the prerequisites are installed successfully on your machine and you have rebooted it, we will publish our Blazor application.

Open the SPAWithBlazor application using Visual Studio 2017.

Right-click on the `SPAWithBlazor.Server` project and click on **Publish**:

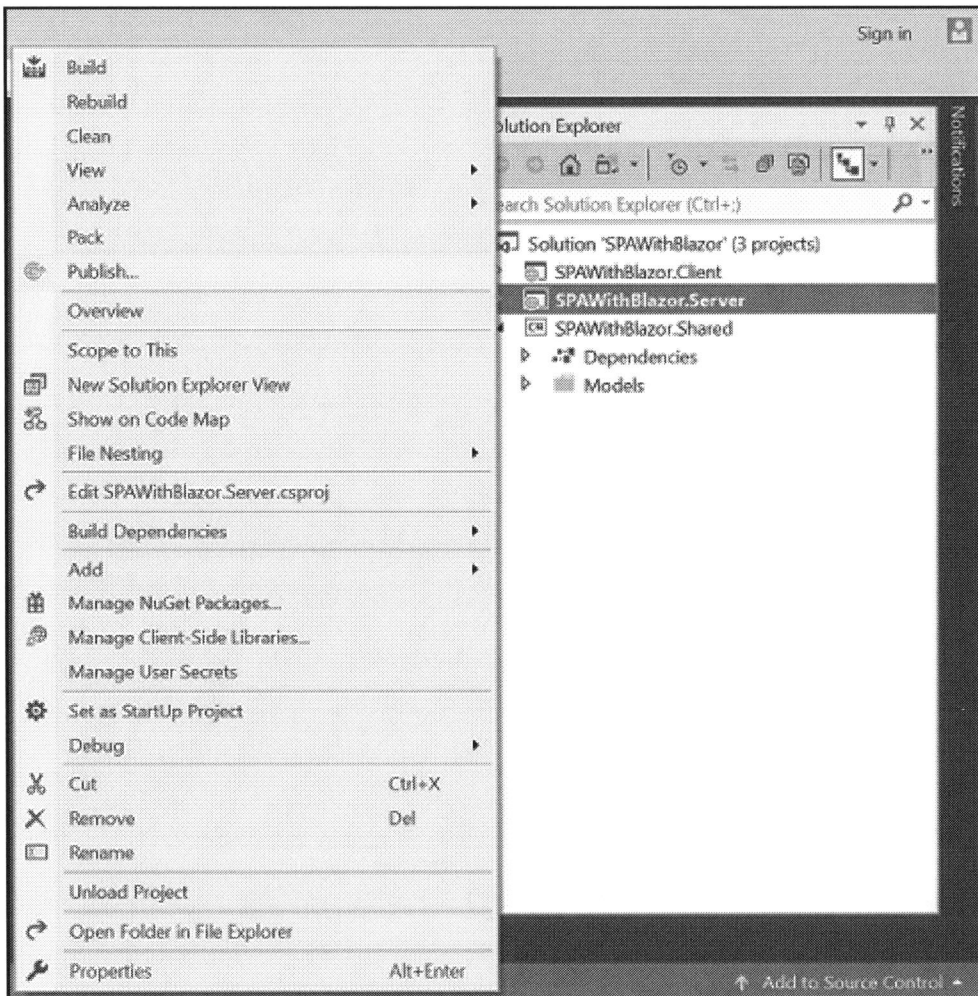

Click on Publish

It will open a window asking you to **Pick a publish target**. Select **Folder** from the left-hand menu and provide the folder path in the given text box. You can provide any folder path where you want to publish your app. Refer to the screenshot below:

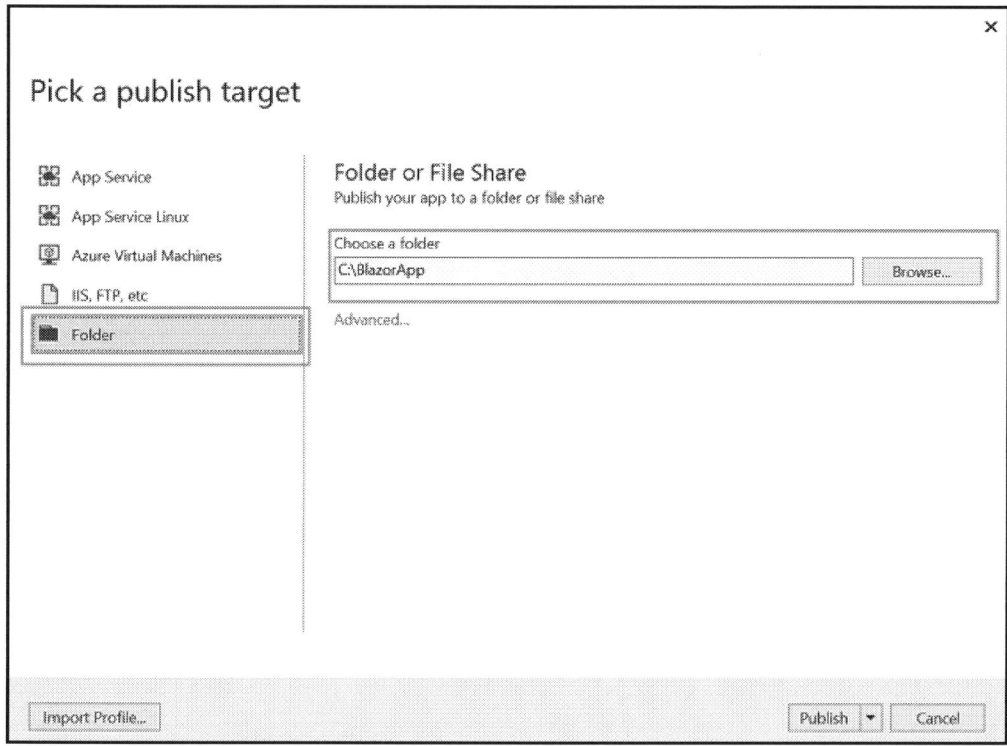

Picking a publishing target

Click on the **Publish** button. Visual Studio will start publishing your application. If there are no build errors, then your application will be published successfully in the specified folder.

After the publishing is successful, we will configure the IIS.

Configuring IIS

Open the `Run` window in your machine and put `inetmgr` in the text box and press **OK** to open the IIS:

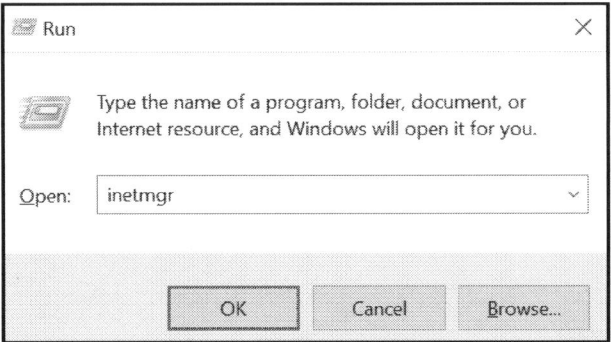

Once the IIS is open, right-click on **Sites | Add Web Site**.

An **Add Website** window will open. Here, we need to furnish details in three fields as mentioned:

- **Site name**: This is your site name. You can put a name as per your choice. Here, we will use **BlazorSPA.**
- **Physical path**: We will provide the path of the folder where the application is published.
- **Host name**: This is the URL for our application.. Here, we will use **SPAWithBlazor.com.**

Click on **OK** to create the website:

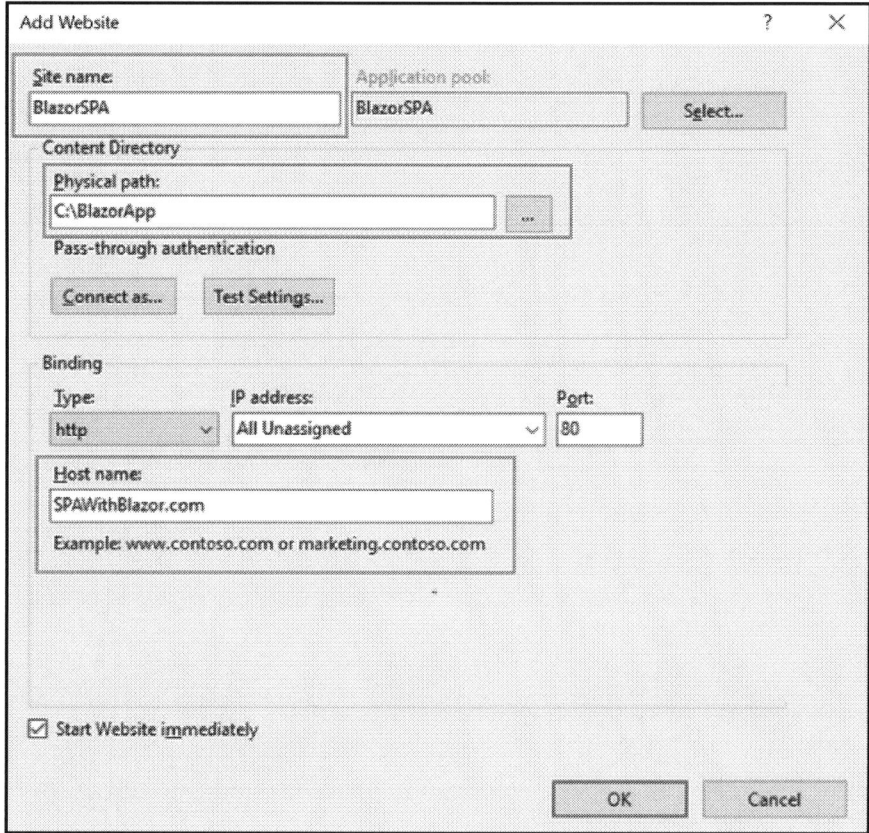

We will configure the **Application Pool**. The name of the application pool is same as the **Site name** we put in the last step. Here, the application pool name will be **BlazorSPA**.

To configure the application pool, follow these steps:

1. Click on **Application Pools** in the panel on the left.
2. Double-click on the pool name **BlazorSPA**.
3. An **Edit Application Pool** window will open.
4. Select the **No Managed Code** option from the .NET CLR version drop-down list. Click **OK**.

Refer to this screenshot:

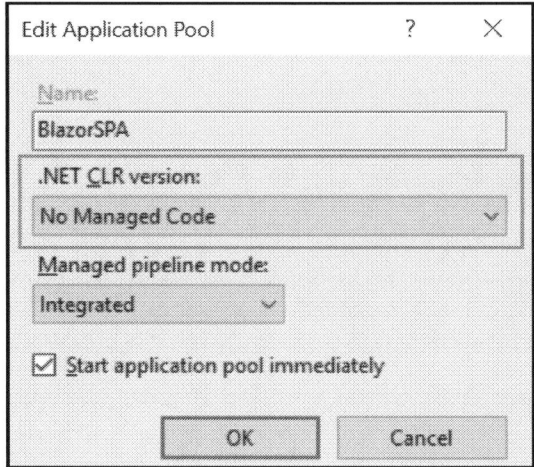

Configuring the DNS host

The final step is to configure our DNS host file.

Navigate to the path C:\Windows\System32\drivers\etc in your machine and open the **hosts** file using any text editor:

We will add the hostname that we provided in IIS against our localhost IP address. Here, the hostname is **SPAWithBlazor.com**.

Refer to this screenshot:

```
1   # Copyright (c) 1993-2009 Microsoft Corp.
2   #
3   # This is a sample HOSTS file used by Microsoft TCP/IP for Windows.
4   #
5   # This file contains the mappings of IP addresses to host names. Each
6   # entry should be kept on an individual line. The IP address should
7   # be placed in the first column followed by the corresponding host name.
8   # The IP address and the host name should be separated by at least one
9   # space.
10  #
11  # Additionally, comments (such as these) may be inserted on individual
12  # lines or following the machine name denoted by a '#' symbol.
13  #
14  # For example:
15  #
16  #      102.54.94.97     rhino.acme.com          # source server
17  #       38.25.63.10     x.acme.com              # x client host
18
19  # localhost name resolution is handled within DNS itself.
20  #   127.0.0.1       localhost
21  #   ::1             localhost
22      127.0.0.1       SPAWithBlazor.com  <----------]  Add this line
23
```

Our Blazor application is successfully hosted and configured. We will now access it via the browser.

Execution demo

Open any browser on your machine. Put in the hostname as the URL, which is **SPAWithBlazor.com**, and press *Enter*. You can see that our application will load in the browser. Click on the **Employee Data** link on the menu on the left, and you can see a page similar to the one shown. You can perform the CRUD operations as we discussed in the previous chapter:

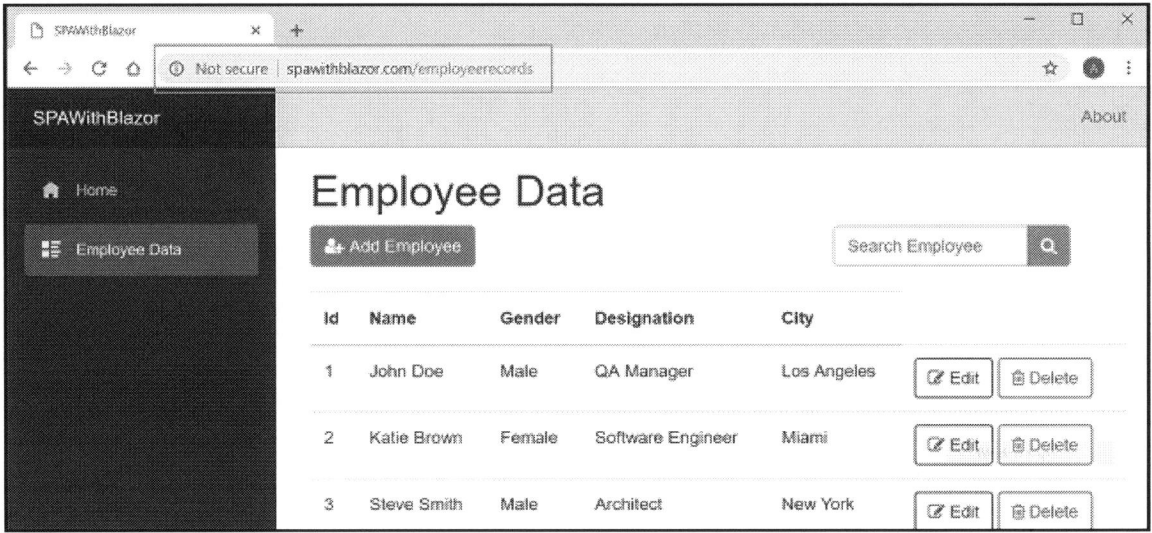

Employee Data

Troubleshoot IIS hosting issues

While hosting a Blazor application on IIS, you might come across some issues. Some of the common hosting issues and their solutions are discussed here:

- The website is not loading and you get a DNS not found error

Verify whether the host file is configured properly. Disconnect any VPN you are using and if you are using any web proxy, then disable it.

- **HTTP Error 500.19**: Internal server error—the requested page cannot be accessed because the related configuration data for the page is invalid

The error message states that the website data is not accessible because of insufficient permissions. You need to allow the IIS_IUSRS group to access the Web.config file by providing it with read permissions on the publish folder.

- The data is not being displayed on the screen, and you get a 500 internal server error on the browser console

Ensure that the connection string you provided is correct. Make sure that the username you put in the connection string has the db_datareader and db_datawriter permissions. If you are still facing the same issue, then provide your user db_owner permission.

- The data is not being displayed on the screen, and you get a operation not allowed error on the browser console

We need to change the IIS setup configuration to resolve this issue.

Open the **Windows Features** window by navigating to **Control Panel | Programs and Features | Turn Windows feature on or off**. Further, navigate to **Internet Information Services | World Wide Web Services | Common HTTP Features** and uncheck the **WebDAV Publishing** option. Click **OK**:

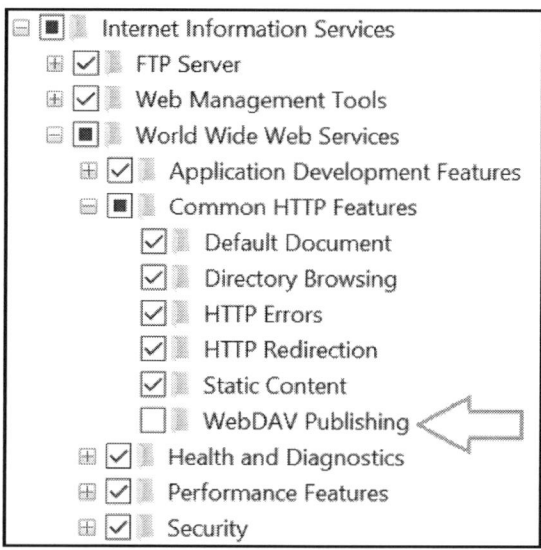

- If you republish the application, then do not forget to refresh your website as well as the application pool in IIS

Deploying the Blazor app on Azure

We will deploy our SPAWithBlazor application on to Azure cloud. You need to have an Azure subscription to host a website on Azure.

You can create a free Azure account at `https://azure.microsoft.com/en-in/free/`

Follow the steps mentioned to host a Blazor app on Azure.

Creating a resource group

The first step is to create a resource group that will contain all our required resources. If you want to use an existing resource group, then you can skip this step.

Open the Azure portal and click on **Resource groups** on the left-hand menu and then click on **Add**. It will open a window asking you to fill out the details for a new resource group:

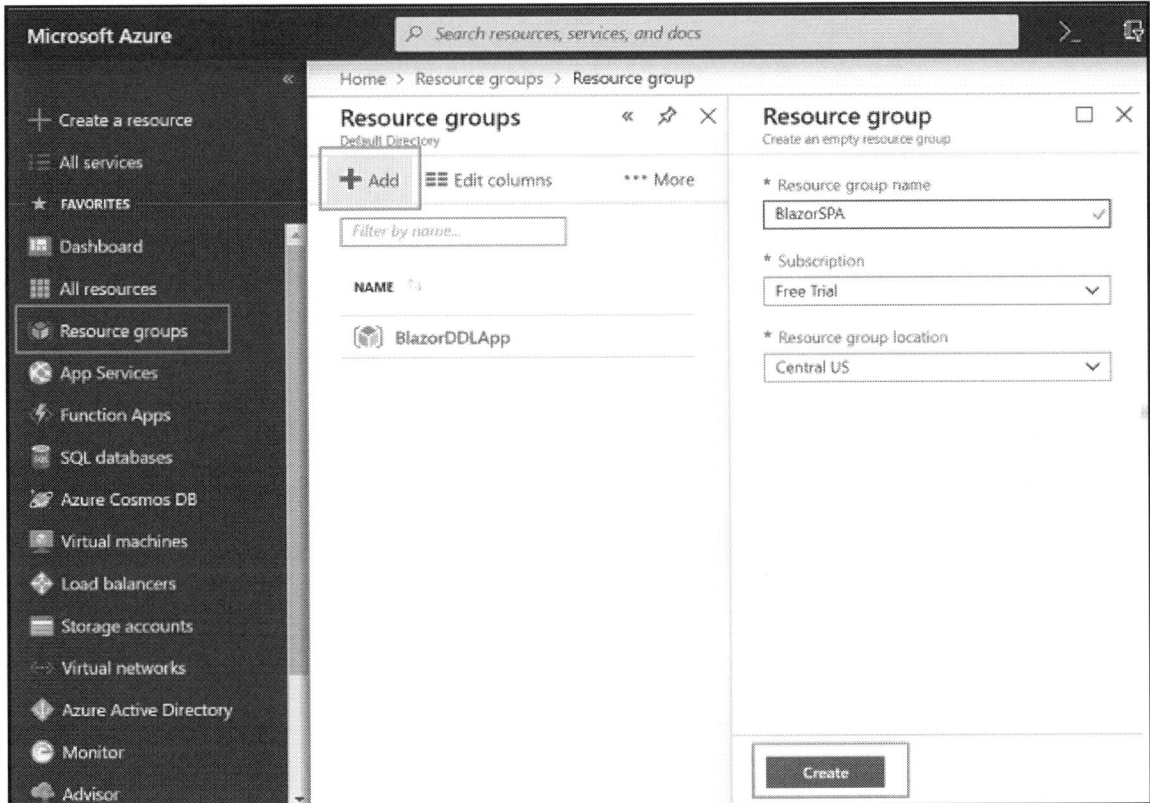

You can use any name as **Resource group name**. I have given the name BlazorSPA. Select your subscription type from the drop-down list. Here I am using a free trial subscription. Select a **Resource group location** from the drop-down list and click on the **Create** button to create an empty resource group.

Creating database objects

We will create a SQL database and a database server on Azure portal. We will then create our tables and stored procedures on the database server.

Creating a SQL database and database server

Click on **SQL databases** on the left-hand menu of the Azure portal and then click **Add**. It will open a window asking you to create a new SQL database:

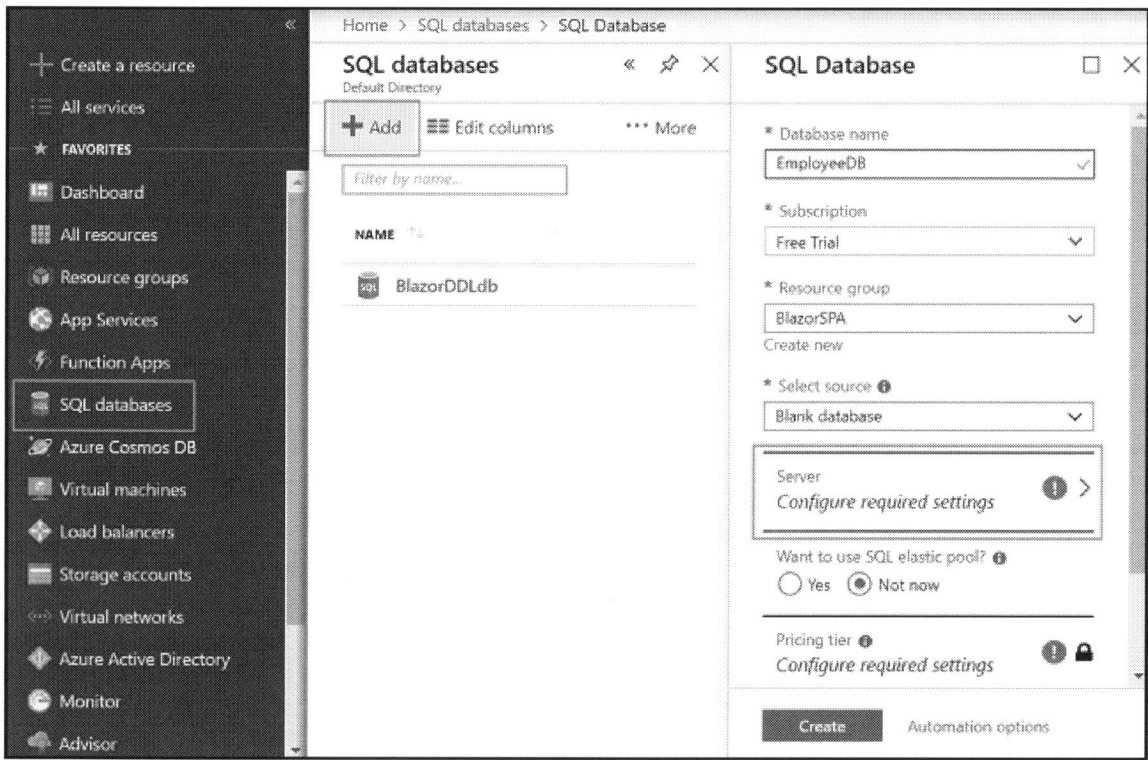

Creating a new SQL database

Give the name of database as `EmployeeDB` and select your subscription type from the drop-down menu. Select your resource group name and then select **Blank database** from the **Select source** drop-down list. To create the database, we need to click on **Create** button, but before that we will create a database server for our SQL database.

Click on the **Server configure required settings** and then click **Create a new server**. It will open a window for creating a new server:

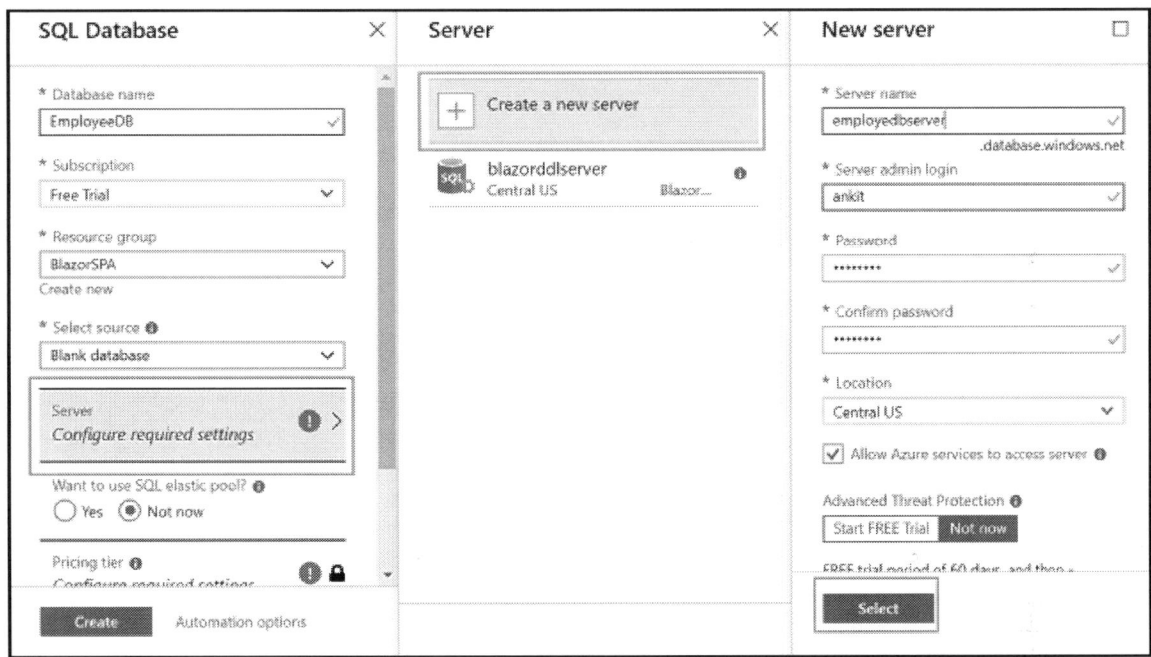

Creating a new server

Give a **Server name** of your choice. Here I am using `employedbserver` as my server name. The DB server will be created by appending `.database.windows.net` to the user-provided server name. Enter a **Server admin login** and **password**, and then click **Select**. It will create a new server for your database. Click on the **Create** button in the **SQL Database** window to create your database.

 The word *admin* is not allowed as the administrator username for the database server.

Creating DB tables and stored procedures

We have created the SQL database and server on Azure, but the database does not have the tables and stored procedures we are using in our application. To create these DB objects, we will connect to Azure database using **SQL Server Management Studio (SSMS)**.

Open SSMS and put the server name as `employedbserver.database.windows.net`. Provide the admin user ID and password that you configured in the previous section and click on **Connect**.

You will get a pop-up window asking you to configure the firewall rule to access your Azure database. Log in with your Azure account credentials and add your machine IP address under **Firewall rule**. Click on **OK** to connect to the Azure database server:

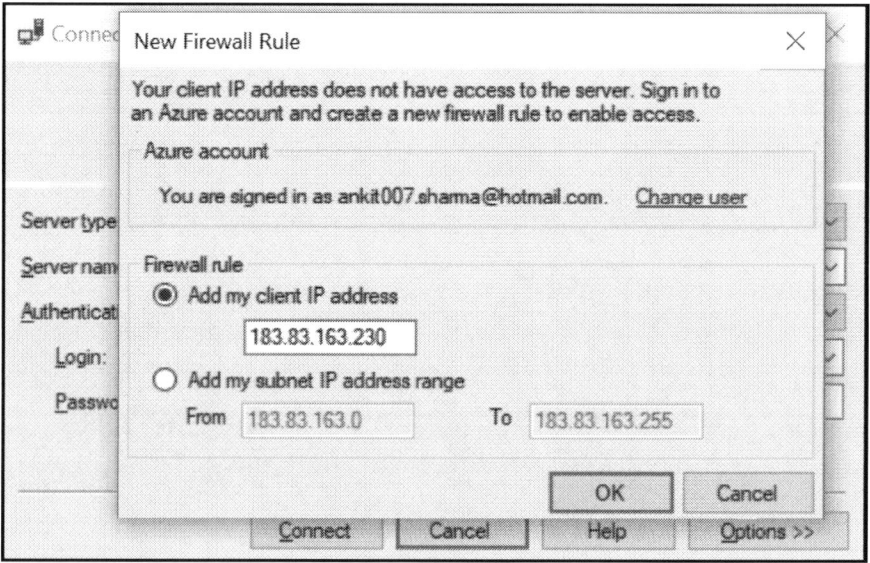

Connecting to Azure database server

After the connection is successful, you can see the `EmployeeDB` database on the server. You need to run the SQL commands discussed in `Chapter 5`, *Creating a Single Page Application Using Blazor* inside the `EmployeeDB` database to create all the tables and stored procedures, which we are using in our application.

Setting the DB connection string

To be able to use the SQL database created on Azure, we have to replace our local connection string in the application with the connection string of the Azure database.

Follow these steps to get the connection string of the Azure database:

1. Open the Azure portal and click on the **SQL databases** option in the menu on the left.
2. A new view will open that will display the list of all your SQL databases on Azure. Select `EmployeeDB` database from the list.
3. Click on **connection strings** on the left-hand menu.
4. Select the **ADO.NET** tab from the window. You can see your connection string on the screen:

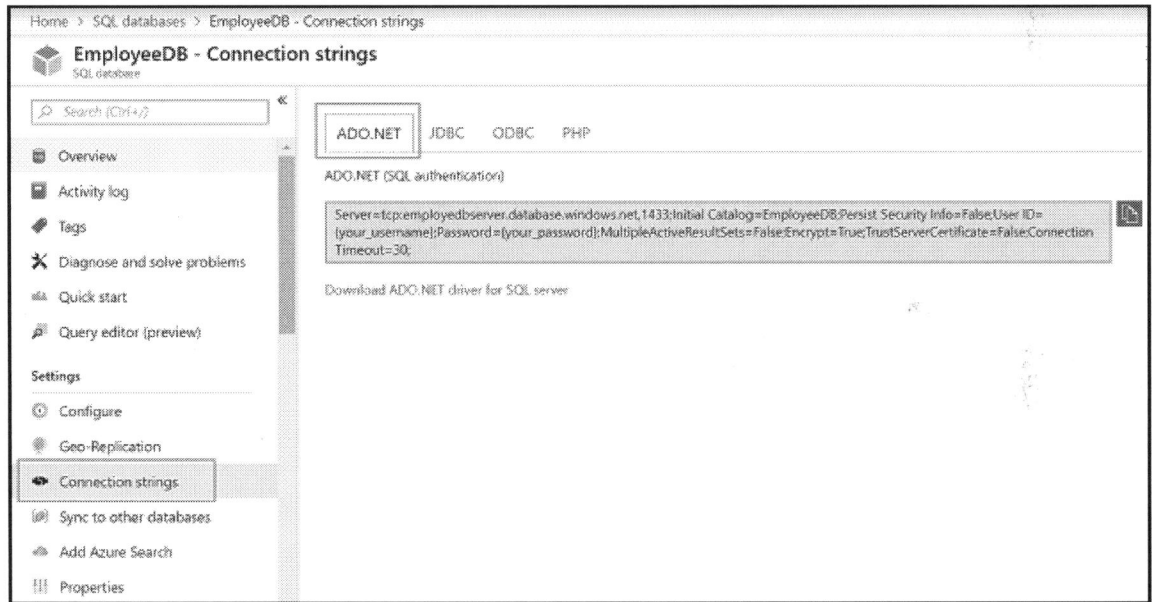

Setting a DB connection string

Put the SQL server admin login and password in the connection string. Open the `SPAWithBlazor` application and replace your connection string with the new connection string.

Before proceeding further, we need to verify whether the connections string is configured correctly and we are able to access Azure database. Execute the application using Visual Studio and verify whether all the operations are working as expected.

Publishing application to Azure

We are now ready to publish our application to Azure.

Open the SPAWithBlazor application using Visual Studio 2017. Right-click on the SPAWithBlazor.Server project and click on **Publish**.

It will open a window asking you to **Pick a publish target**. Select **App Service** from the left-hand menu. Select **Create New** radio button and click on **Create profile**:

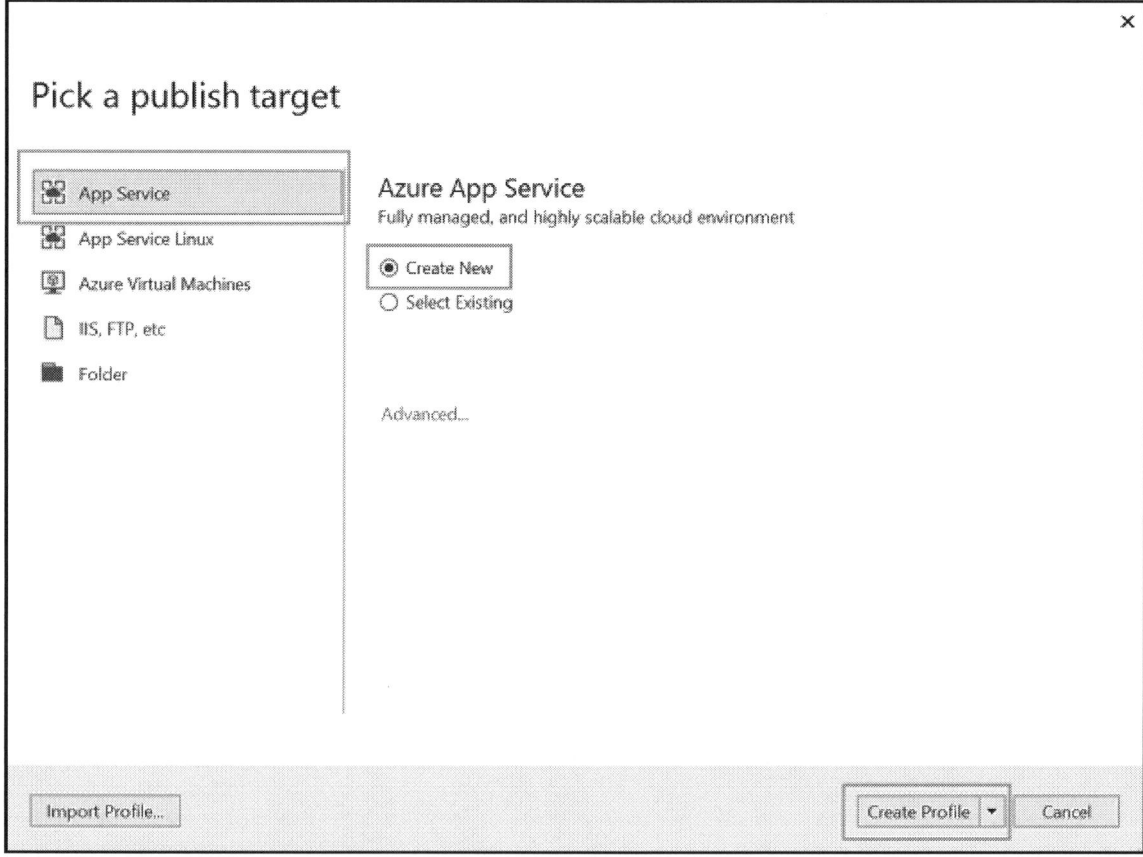

If you are not signed into your Azure account from Visual Studio, you will be prompted to log into Azure. After the successful login, a **Create App Service** window will open:

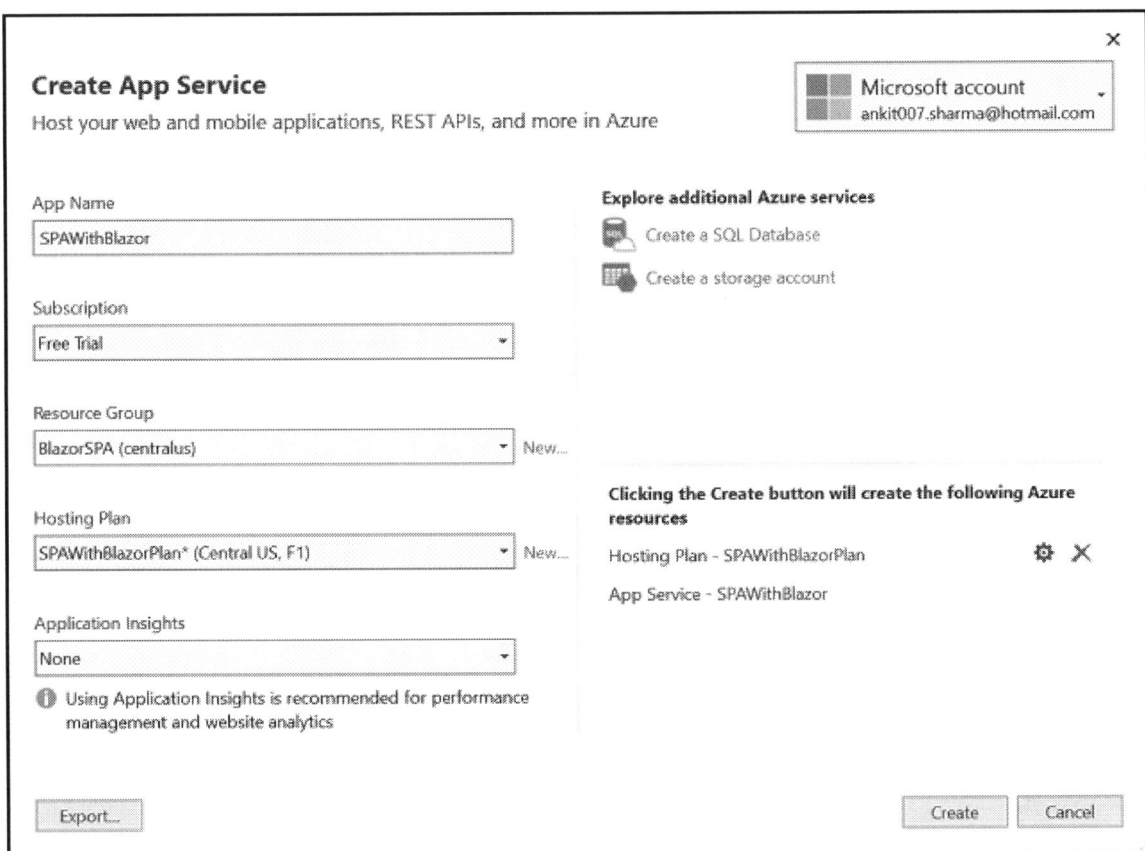

The fields in this window are prepopulated, but you can change them as per your requirement. Fill out the details as mentioned:

- **App Name**: Give any name of your choice. The website's public URL will be app name followed by `.azurewebsites.net`. Here, I am using the name as `SPAWithBlazor`, hence the URL of the app will be `SPAWithBlazor.azurewebsites.net`.
- **Subscription**: Select your Azure subscription type.
- **Resource Group**: Select the resource group name that we created earlier.
- **Hosting Plan**: This is your web-hosting plan. If you want to change this, click on the **New...** link and select a new plan.

- **Application Insights**: Select a value from drop-down list. This is useful in website performance management and analytics.

Clicking on **Create** will start the application deployment on Azure. It will take a few minutes, depending on your internet connection speed.

If the application is deployed successfully, click on the **Publish** button. It will publish your app to Azure. When the app publish is successful, Visual Studio will launch the website in your machine's browser. Alternatively, you can also open the website by visiting SPAWithBlazor.azurewebsites.net from any browser in your machine.

You can see the application home page as shown here:

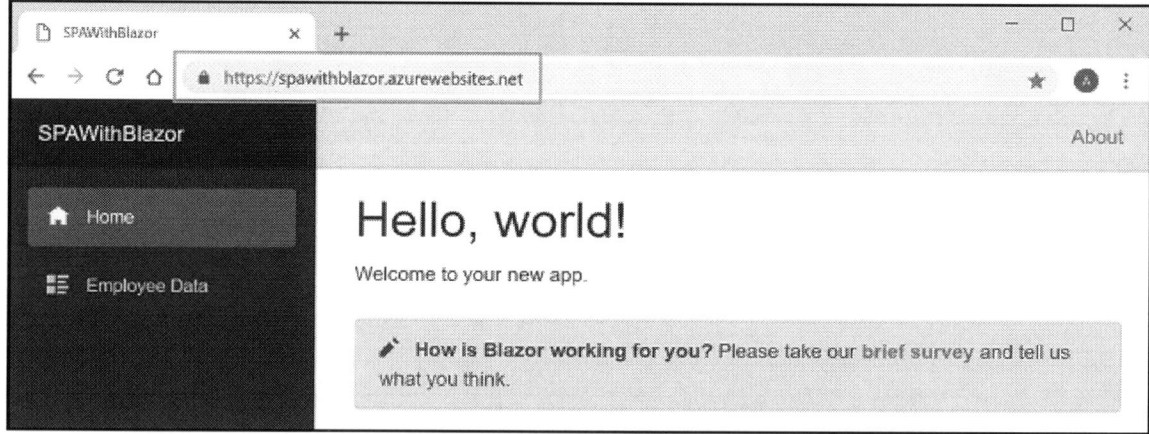

The Application homepage

Summary

In this chapter, we learned how to deploy a Blazor application. We configured IIS on a Windows 10 machine and deployed our Blazor application on it. We also learned about troubleshooting a few of the common hosting issues with IIS.

We learned about deploying and publishing a Blazor application on an Azure cloud. We have created a SQL server database on Azure and configured it to use as the database provider for our application.

Other Books You May Enjoy

If you enjoyed this book, you may be interested in these other books by Packt:

ASP.NET Core 2 and Angular 5
Valerio De Sanctis

ISBN: 9781788293600

- Use ASP.NET Core to its full extent to create a versatile backend layer based on RESTful APIs
- Consume backend APIs with the brand new Angular 5 HttpClient and use RxJS Observers to feed the frontend UI asynchronously
- Implement an authentication and authorization layer using ASP.NET Identity to support user login with integrated and third-party OAuth 2 providers
- Configure a web application in order to accept user-defined data and persist it into the database using server-side APIs
- Secure your application against threats and vulnerabilities in a time efficient way
- Connect different aspects of the ASP. NET Core framework ecosystem and make them interact with each other for a Full-Stack web development experience

Learn WebAssembly
Mike Rourke

ISBN: 9781788997379

- Learn how WebAssembly came to be and its associated elements (text format, module, and JavaScript API)
- Create, load, and debug a WebAssembly module (editor and compiler/toolchain)
- Build a high-performance application using C and WebAssembly
- Extend WebAssembly's feature set using Emscripten by porting a game written in C++
- Explore upcoming features of WebAssembly, Node.js integration, and alternative compilation methods

Leave a review - let other readers know what you think

Please share your thoughts on this book with others by leaving a review on the site that you bought it from. If you purchased the book from Amazon, please leave us an honest review on this book's Amazon page. This is vital so that other potential readers can see and use your unbiased opinion to make purchasing decisions, we can understand what our customers think about our products, and our authors can see your feedback on the title that they have worked with Packt to create. It will only take a few minutes of your time, but is valuable to other potential customers, our authors, and Packt. Thank you!

Index

C

C# code
  JavaScript function, calling from 57
C# method
  calling, from JavaScript code 66, 68, 70, 71
calculator app, Blazor
  component, creating 91
  executing 94, 95
  logic, adding 93
  UI, creating 91, 93
calculator app
  creating, with Blazor 90
code
  adding, to component 120
Command-Line Interface (CLI) 7
Common Language Runtime (CLR) 9
component
  code, adding 120
  EmployeeData.cshtml file, coding 124, 126, 128
  EmployeeData.cshtml.cs file, coding 120, 122, 123
  in Blazor 31
  navigation link, adding 128

D

data access layer
  creating, for Blazor application 105
data binding, Blazor
  one-way data binding 38
  two-way data binding 38, 40
data binding
  in Blazor 37
database objects
  creating 98
  stored procedures, creating 99
  table, creating 98
dependency injection
  in Blazor 48, 49

E

EF Core's database-first approach
  used, for scaffolding model 104
EF Core, for data access
  employee record, adding 106

  employee record, deleting 107
  employee record, fetching 105, 107
  employee record, updating 106
  list of cities, fetching 108
EF Core
  used, for accessing data 105
Entity Framework (EF) 97
event handling
  in Blazor 41, 42

H

HTML elements
  references, capturing 63, 64, 66

I

IIS, Blazor app deployment
  .NET Core hosting bundle, installing 137, 138
  DNS host, configuring 143
  execution demo 144
  hosting issues, troubleshooting 145, 146
  Internet Information Services (IIS), configuring 141, 142
  Internet Information Services (IIS), installing 136
  prerequisites 136
  URL rewrite module, installing 136
Internet Information Services (IIS)
  about 136
  Blazor app, deploying 135
  Blazor app, publishing to 138, 140

J

JavaScript (JS) 117
JavaScript code
  C# method, calling from 66, 68, 70, 71
JavaScript function
  calling, from C# code 57
  calling, with parameters 60, 61, 62
  calling, without parameters 59, 60
JavaScript Interop 56
JavaScript methods
  defining 58
JS Interop
  references, adding for 119

L

layouts
  in Blazor 46, 47

N

navigation link
  adding, to component 128

R

raw HTML
  rendering 52, 53
references
  adding, for JS Interop 119
  capturing, to HTML elements 63, 64, 66
routing, Blazor
  navigation, between components 50, 51
  NavLink component 51, 52
  parameterized routing 50
routing
  in Blazor 49

S

Single Page Application (SPA) 7, 77, 97, 117
SQL Server Management Studio (SSMS) 150
stored procedures
  cities record, fetching 100

employee record, adding 99
employee record, deleting 100
employee record, fetching 100
employee record, updating 99

T

third-party JS libraries
  using 72, 73, 75
Tic-Tac-Toe game application, Blazor
  components, creating 81, 82
  executing 87, 89, 90
  logic, implementing 82, 84
  navigation link, adding 86
  UI, creating 85
Tic-Tac-Toe game application
  creating, with Blazor 79, 81

V

Visual Studio (VS) 77, 97, 117
VS 2017
  installation link 78
  used, for creating Blazor application 101, 103
  used, for setting up Blazor development
    environment 78

W

WebAssembly 9

Printed in Great Britain
by Amazon